DEVOTIONAL COLLECTION

80 Christian Devotions About God's Love And Acceptance

Mona Hanna

Devotional Collection
Copyright © 2012 by Mona Hanna

ISBN-10: 1480105465
ISBN-13: 978-1480105461

All Scripture quotations, unless otherwise indicated, are taken from the HOLY BIBLE, NEW INTERNATIONAL VERSION® NIV®. Copyright © 1973, 1978, 1984 by International Bible Society®. Used by permission of International Bible Society®. All rights reserved worldwide.

"NIV" and "NEW INTERNATIONAL VERSION" are trademarks registered in the United States Patent and Trademark Office by International Bible Society®.

All rights reserved. No part of this literary work may be reproduced in any form or by any means — electronic, mechanical, photocopy, recording, or any other — without the prior written consent of the author, except for brief quotations used in reviews.

Books by Mona Hanna

The Nature of God: 50 Christian Devotions about God's Love and Acceptance

God's Promises of Love: 30 Christian Devotions about God's Love and Acceptance

THE NATURE OF GOD - BOOK 1

God Knows Me	1
Relationship	2
No Matter What	3
The Nature of God	4
He Just Wants Me to Be Happy	6
How We Pray	7
Faith	8
His Love Is Personal	9
Protecting Me	11
God Is in Control	12
Not Alone	13
Small Things	14
Our Sadness	15
Letter to God	16
Always Listens	17
Jesus Loved Us First	18
God Holds Onto Us	20
God Has a Plan	21
Tell Him Everything	22
God Has His Own Goals	23
He Wants to Heal Us	24
We're Not Trapped	25
The Real God	26
How Good He Is	27
Jesus Owns My Life	28

Nothing Can Separate Us	29
Putting God First	30
God Will Carry Us	31
God's Love Is Genuine	32
God Accepts Us	33
We're Here with a Purpose	34
Be With Him Out of Love	35
God Gives to Us	36
We're Not Failing	37
Only God Can Make Me Love Him	38
It's God's Job to Change Me	40
God Eases the Pressure We Feel	41
God Sees Our Pain	42
God Will Help Us	43
When God Is Quiet	44
God on Our Side	46
God Is My Strength	48
Taking Care of Others	50
Feeling Guilty over Our Focus	52
God Is Only about Love	54
The Loveliness of God	56
We Don't Have a Divine Duty	57
When We're Lonely	59
We Belong Here	60
We're Doing What We Can	62

GOD'S PROMISES OF LOVE - BOOK 2

Even if I Do Something Wrong, on Purpose	67
We Don't Need to Have Perfect Faith	68
God is Always With Us	69
We Can Be Weak	71
God Doesn't Judge Us	72
We're Not on Our Own	73
What God Has Done With His Love	74
God is With Us, Even if We Feel Badly	76
Jesus Controls Our Pain	78
Comfort When We Fail	80
We're Forgiven	82
God Isn't Disappointed In Us	83
We Don't Have an Obligation	84
God Sees Every Part of Me	86
God Wants to Heal Our Relationships	88
God's Expectations	89
Why It Has to Rain	90
Jesus Sees Everything That's Good About Us	92
The Question of Church	94
God Doesn't Pressure Us	96
God is Only About Love	98
God is Our Closest Friend	100
Jesus Sees Us as Blameless	102
We're Acceptable Because of Jesus	103
Jesus Understands Our Sin	105
God is Proud of How We Work	107
God Controls Our Lives	108
Jesus Will Always Forgive Us	109
How Much Jesus Loves You	110
God Will Change Our Lives	112

The Nature of God

Book 1

God Knows Me

God knows every inch of me.

He made me. He created me. He made my mind. My heart. My soul. My talents. All of me.

He knows *everything* I worry about, and looks at me with love and compassion.

He sits with me always, right beside me, protecting me.

I don't have to struggle alone, waiting until I'm "good" or in a "place of understanding about God" to pray.

I can talk to him anytime. He wants to hear from me. He loves me. I don't have to wait to talk to him — I can talk to him now.

He'll never leave me, loves me more than life itself. *I am not alone.*

RELATIONSHIP

At times I feel an ache, an inner loneliness that cripples me.

But I forget about God. I forget that God loves me, and actually wants a relationship with me.

A Christian friend of mine told me that God has emotions. Not that he's defensive and unstable, but he loves me and is sad when I turn away from him. He feels sadness when I'm hurt, and feels love and joy at my happiness.

I matter to him. He isn't an emotionless deity, watching from afar and not caring. He doesn't go about his plans without caring if I'm involved. What I do matters to him. What I say matters. How I treat him. If I spend time with him.

He loves me, and just as I would be hurt if someone I love rejected me, he's hurt when I reject him. Just as I feel sad when someone I love is sad, or I'm in pain when they're upset — God's the same. He aches when I'm upset. He actually loves me. He cries when I cry. If only I could see it. Any pain I feel would be diminished in light of God's love. He cares about every part of me. If only I could see it.

No Matter What

I often feel that God's love is fallible — that if I do the wrong thing, or make a mess of my life, he'll love me less. I tell myself yes, God loves me, but he won't accept me if I do something awful, or continually make mistakes. If I don't understand him, and fail, he'll look away.

But if we look at the Bible, we see even the greatest people, who God loved and changed the world through, made some terrible mistakes. Look at David. God loved him with all his heart, and was enormously proud of him. But David fell down, and committed adultery and murder. He had many great insights about God, but even he didn't always see God clearly. Yet God still loved him. He didn't look away from him. He didn't reject him. And David went on to be one of the greatest people in history, because of the works God performed through him.

In our own lives, it's okay to make mistakes and be confused, anxious and stressed. It's normal and God still loves us. He's with us no matter what — no matter what we do, even if we feel foolish and ashamed. He doesn't see us the way we see ourselves. He's with us even if we don't understand him, and totally fall apart. It's not a requirement of our relationship with God to never fall down. Jesus died to connect us to God despite our failures, and there are no barriers we could possibly create that could break that bond. God will always love us. No matter what.

The Nature of God

One of my biggest struggles with Christianity is feeling that God is upset with me.

When I first became a Christian, I didn't understand God at all, so naturally my faith was very limited. All I knew was that I wanted to be in a relationship with him. I did my best to not give up, and I took very small steps to grow closer to him. Eventually, over many months, he showed me he loved me, and taught me to love myself.

In my current relationship with God, when something goes wrong, I can become confused and upset. I can feel he led me somewhere only for me to get hurt, or I can be confused by the messages I feel he's giving me. But the intense pain I feel during this time is partly because I feel by doubting God, I'm causing a huge rift that even he can't repair. I feel if I don't understand God perfectly, he loves me less, and is no longer protecting me.

But this isn't true. God loves each of us more than we could possibly know, and a loving father would never be angry with us for having doubts. In those initial months of being a Christian, when we didn't understand him at all, was God mad at us? Did he expect us to completely understand him, and become angry with us for being hurt and troubled? Of course not.

Just because our relationship with God has become more mature, it doesn't mean we aren't going to doubt, and God understands this. He still loves and protects us, and will be right by our side while we work through our conflict with him. He hears our every prayer. We feel ashamed for doubting him and for being ungrateful, but God knows our nature. He'll never look away from us, and is always at work in our lives, even when we can't see it. God loves us. There's nothing a human could do to change the nature of God.

He Just Wants Me to Be Happy

I had a moment, in which I glimpsed the depth of God's love for me. All my preconceived notions were wiped away.

I saw that God is sweet and kind, and truly wants me to be happy, because he loves me. He isn't trying to teach me certain lessons because I *should* go through them, and he's demanding them. He just wants me to be happy. It's not about fulfilling a certain number of tasks, or "proving my faith" — he loves me like a parent loves a child, and wants me to be happy and content inside.

He doesn't judge me, and think I'm "bad" for maybe being selfish and not thinking of him first or exactly right. He doesn't frown upon me for praying about a certain thing, even if I pray a lot — even if I feel stupid. He loves me to talk to him. He listens every time. He cares about me more than I could ever know, and his loves fills me up like nothing else can.

Even if I can't find a man to love me, God will, and his love is all I need. He'll be with me every moment, and understands all my heartache.

In *no way* does God judge me the way I judge myself. In no way does he place that pressure on me. He loves me. He loves me.

How We Pray

We pray to God as if he's judging us, and has specific rules and guidelines for us to follow. We don't pray to him as if he's a loving father, who only has our best interests at heart. We pray to God with an image of him in our heads — negative images made up of our own judgments of him, and the words and writings of others who tell us what God expects. We feel closer to a friend of ours who is loving and accepts us, than we do to God. We can tell the friend anything. But God will judge us.

But we need to wipe this image of God out of our minds. God is kinder, sweeter, more patient, more loving, more accepting and more understanding than any person could be. God is a loving father, and our relationship with him is a relationship, not a servant blindly following their master. We shouldn't see God as a concept — a set of rules and guidelines we should adapt because others tell us to.

God is your best friend — your confidant, your father, the one who truly knows you. You'll never find a person who loves you as much as God does. Don't fear he's judging you. Don't fear he's upset with you. Wipe every harsh notion you have of God out of your mind. God accepts you more than any human on earth ever could. Pray to him as if he loves you so much, he would die for you. Just imagine he loves you that much.

Faith

Once, a Christian friend of mine said something to me about faith. She said the promises God has made to us are always true, no matter how we're feeling. Unfortunately, this is something I find hard to remember.

God has said a great many things to me over the years since I became a Christian. He's said my life is his now. He's said he would take care of my entire Christian journey — he would do everything. He's said that, even though he desperately didn't want to go through with the crucifixion, he did it because he loves me so very, very much. And God has said he's proud of me — not because I do everything right, or achieve great things, but because I try hard and I mean well.

And yet so often I feel sad and alone, and forget everything I've been told. I've struggled with depression since I was 17, and so frequently I have to deal with negative thinking and insecurity. I can feel that I'm completely on my own, and that my life has no direction or purpose.

But everything God has ever said to me is still true. I am not alone. God does love me. Jesus himself is guiding my Christian journey, and will never leave me, or look away.

Even if I'm lost and understand little else, I can hold onto God's promises. Where I stand with God is not based on how I feel. I can't assume that God loves me less, or is protecting me less, if I feel awful or am going through a difficult situation. And, most importantly, God doesn't keep his promises to me based on how "good" a Christian I am, but because Jesus died for my sins, and paid for everything I do wrong.

So I need to hold onto the beautiful things God has said to me. He will never let me down. I need to have faith.

His Love Is Personal

I learned something about God's love a while ago, when I was having a difficult time at work. He said to me that I couldn't do my job any better, because I was dedicated and I meant well. I was doing my best, so that's all I could do. It was as if God was smiling at me, and proud of me.

A wave of love washed over me. I realized that God's love for me is personal — he cares about me as an individual. He doesn't love me because he has to. He loves me like a loving parent would — is proud of me when I'm trying, and is moved when I truly say sorry. His love is not neutral, as if he sees all people the same way. He sees every aspect of my life, right down to the last detail.

I usually think God is ashamed of me and can't look at me because I'm a "bad Christian." But God cares about me and what I do. He's sad when I'm upset. Just because I don't hear him straight away when I cry out, doesn't mean he's not upset and feeling for me. He's *truly* loving, and there are no rules or laws that can ever separate us.

I'm not alone anymore, and fighting the world on my own. I finally have someone who loves me. And he always will, no matter what I do, even if I don't understand him. He gave up his life for me. Personally.

God holds onto me, and will bring me where I need to be. He'll heal my heart, far beyond my attempts to heal myself. It's alright when I'm hurting. He's holding me, even if I'm not looking at him and can't see it.

God asks so little of us. We only need to accept Jesus as our savior, ask him to be with us, and make small steps to slowly include God in our lives. What he gives us will always far outweigh what we could ever give him. God's love is personal, for everyone. He cares deeply about every single person, not based on how good they are, or what they've done — but because God is love. Just ask him to be with you. It's all he wants.

PROTECTING ME

It's God. It's God who's protecting me. He knows what he's doing! It's God himself. He doesn't do things badly. He doesn't "drop the ball." He doesn't do things *less* because I'm a "bad Christian" or I don't believe. He *is* in control. If I were out on the street, he'd be with me. He'd protect me. It's *God*. He doesn't love me less or *care* for me less because I make mistakes. He has a plan and I'm part of it, and he doesn't look away or become less active. He loves me just as much as he loves anyone else. He loves me.

So trust him. I love him. He's perfect.

God Is In Control

I will take heart. I will be at rest. God is in control of my life. Even if bad things happen, he's with me. Even if I don't know what to do, he does. God will guide me to where he wants me to be, and he'll guide me to do what he wants me to do.

Part of this journey may involve pain and suffering, and feeling lost and anxious and afraid. But God is with me in all those moments. I don't feel "bad" because I'm far from God or failing him. My pain is part of my journey, and God is in control of that too.

I don't have to decide every facet of my future. I just have to keep going, and God will give me things to do. I may come to realize what to do after a time of confusion. I may still be confused and just try to do something — anything — to move forward. The path will eventually lead to God. He'll control that — not me.

My pain is in God's control. My anxiety is in his hands. Seek help for your pain — don't suffer alone if someone can help. Seek out the help of others. But I'm watched, and held, and treasured. I'm protected and part of a plan, and nothing can break that plan. I'm safe and in the mind of God himself. I'm loved, with a love that's greater and more powerful than death itself. I don't have to understand that God's holding me, for him to be doing so. And he is the one who'll teach me.

Not Alone

Is everything okay?

Is everything alright?

Is *nothing* so bad it can't be beaten?

Is the darkest pain, the deepest scar, the coldest day, still in the light?

Is the light brighter and stronger than anything? Than death?

Is he better than anything? He speaks our language. Understands our hearts. Our needs, desires, temptations, evils.

He's so great he saw our evil, our wrong, our separation, and sent his Son to die in the most horrific way, for us.

For us. Can anything be overcome? Is anything beatable? Is there *anything* else we can look at? No. Not love of another, not romance, not career, money, pleasure. Everything can be taken away. Everything can die, go, leave. But not that. Not that. Nothing can take that away, or supersede it. He sees us *as we are*, our deepest hearts and souls, our evils, our wrongs, and he died *for everyone*. No matter how bad, or small.

If we ever wonder if there's a point, if there's any point to our lives — if there's any point in being alive. There's that. He will *never* leave you, loves you more than life itself. There's nothing he can't do, but he'll only do what's good. Let your heart be full. Believe. You're not alone. And never will be.

Small Things

I don't think Christianity is about suddenly being an extremely good person who does everything right, or thinking perfectly or thinking exactly right about God.

I think it's about taking a step of faith and being willing to have a relationship with God, then doing small things, like reading about him, to encourage that relationship. God will do the rest. But we have to do something.

Our Sadness

Our sadness doesn't come from the bad things that are happening to us, or our mistakes.

Our sadness and emptiness comes from not believing we're loved and accepted. When we truly see that God totally loves and accepts us, we feel complete and healed and whole. The answer to every problem lies with him. The healing of every heartache lies with him, not anything else. We don't fix our problems by dealing with the situation on our own, and trying to force an answer. We deal with our problems effectively by turning to God, who offers love and truth and acceptance. Be with God. He will heal you.

Letter to God

Dear God,

Thank you for making me. Thank you that you love me despite my bad thoughts, despite my bad behavior, my anger, my lies, my failures. Thank you that you listen to my every word, no matter how dark or woefully unworthy of you. Thank you that you love me, even though my heart is black. I want to see the truth, live in the truth, not the dark. See the brightness. But not for my pleasure — not so I can feel good and then forget. There's something far brighter and better than my little soul can handle, and I throw my soul away on nothing.

I don't want to do that. I will forget — I will screw up. But the truth will not go away. Help me to always find the truth. In books, in words, in music — however you want to show it to me. I'm deeply selfish and always out for myself, but that's a bad way to live.

Help me to see you, and not myself. Help me to never give up. For you, and not myself. You're brighter than the darkest of days. We're here for you. We should be here for you. We owe you everything. You gave us breath, then made a way for us to be rescued when we descend to madness. You love us more than anything. It would be the *best thing* in the world for me to live how a human was created to live. The true way. I'll fail a million times. I'm failing as I write these words.

I'm sorry. Thank you that you love me. I'll try to love you. I'm sorry if I fail.

Always Listens

I often think God hasn't heard me when I've prayed. When it seems like I haven't gotten a response, I feel like God hasn't listened, or he doesn't think my prayer is important enough. If God truly heard me, he would do something, or say something to me.

But God hears us every time we pray. When he doesn't reply immediately, it doesn't mean he hasn't listened, or we've done something to "distance" ourselves from God. It's not as if he's upset with us, and that's why he's not responding.

God will respond to our prayers when he thinks it's right, and will act in our lives at a pace designed with his love for us at heart. As much as we're concerned for our circumstances, or distraught over the life of another — God is just as concerned, and aware of every detail. He cares more than we ever could, and feels more strongly than we ever could feel.

At all times, God's reasoning for his actions is based on his immense love for us, and his true love for those around us. Remember, when God doesn't respond immediately to our prayers, it's not because we haven't prayed "properly," or that we're separate from God. He hears every word, and will act at the right time. God loves all of us very deeply. Pray to him as much as you can. He always listens.

JESUS LOVED US FIRST

During my years of being a Christian, I've slowly learned about who Jesus is. I've had moments of immense joy, in which I received a glimpse of his love and grace. I've started to appreciate how great a gift his death on the cross is. But there are other times when I feel separate from Jesus, and fearful he's judging me.

Jesus' death on the cross means he's taken the blame for all the things I do wrong in my life, and God won't make me pay for my sins. Jesus has paid the penalty, and I can be free to have a close, loving relationship with God.

But sometimes when I read the gospels, I see Jesus criticizing people, and feel he must be criticizing me also. I forget about his love, and only see words of judgment. I do so much that's wrong. How can Jesus not be frowning upon my dark thoughts, and my many mistakes?

This troubles me, and I feel there's a wall between me and Jesus. But I'm not seeing the truth. I do make a lot of mistakes, and will do so for the rest of my life. I deserve to be judged. But Jesus doesn't frown upon me; he looks at me with love, and warmth, and kindness. For every bad thing I do, Jesus sees the pain that caused me to do it, and longs to heal me. He sees every difficult thing I've been through, and tells me I'm doing the best that I can. He reassures me when I fall down. He tells me I'm not abnormal. And he even listens to me when I scream at him that my life's unfair.

Jesus loves me, and it's not a love dependent on me doing the right thing, or being a good person. He hears my every dark thought, and loves me anyway. He sees every bad thing I've ever done, and loves me anyway.

His love for me can be defined by one thing. He died for me. Someone who loves me that much will never leave me.

He loves me so much he won't judge me, and he died for me so I won't be judged. But he loved me first. Jesus loved us first.

So I shouldn't be upset when I read the Bible. There isn't a wall between me and Jesus, no matter how I feel. He's eternally with me, and loves me with all his heart. I will be safe and protected by his love. He loves me.

God Holds Onto Us

In my walk as a Christian, I often feel I have to understand God perfectly. As much as I can only progress in my Christian journey at the pace God designs, I still feel that I need to understand him extremely well, and sometimes try to "force" concepts of him into my head. I become stressed if I'm unclear about Christianity, or where I am with God.

But a friend once told me that sometimes we can only hold onto God by the smallest amount. She said even if we're just barely holding onto God, that's okay. God holds onto us.

Sometimes we can become confused and overwhelmed in our lives, and find being a Christian very difficult. We admonish ourselves for not doing more, and feel we need to meet a standard of behavior. But God just cares that we try. If we're trying to be with God, but sometimes can only barely hang in there, he understands this. His love covers us completely. All he asks of us in our dark times is to not give up. He won't reject us, or fault us for not doing enough. He sees that we're trying, and loves us for staying with him.

God does so much in our lives, without us even knowing or asking. It's not as if we need to be completely clear about our Christianity, for God to be at work. God will act in our lives according to the plan he's laid out — a plan he's lovingly designed for us individually. We don't have to earn or deserve his love. He'll do things for us because he loves us, and is eternally connected to us because of Jesus' loving sacrifice.

So just do what you can, as a Christian. Even if all you're doing is not giving up. God asks for a commitment, but this can be small, and fragile. God will never ask more of us than we're able to give. He'll hold onto us in our relationship with him, and will bring us to a place of greater understanding in his perfect timing.

God Has a Plan

I'm not alone. God has a plan for me. He doesn't ask that I know everything. He doesn't ask that I don't make mistakes. He just asks that I try in my life, and try to be with him.

I feel despair at my circumstances; at my endless failures and seemingly hopeless situation. I feel anxiety and fear and doubt — I feel so very afraid and hopeless. I feel I've failed, and am doing everything wrong. But my future is not lost. My future is not in my control — it's controlled by God. If I make a million mistakes, the plan for my life isn't ruined, because it's designed by God, and he knows what he's doing. He's planned every step, with who I am in mind.

God loves me. My life is carefully managed by him. All he asks is I try, no matter how I feel. I can feel horrible, and still be doing the right thing. God just asks that I try, and try to believe in him. He loves me. I know he loves me. He always has. He always will.

TELL HIM EVERYTHING

God doesn't care how much we pray to him about something. We can pray about the same thing a hundred times, and he doesn't mind. He's not upset with us for not having enough faith. He just wants to hear from us. He's happy for us to talk to him about anything, anytime. He doesn't want us to be fake with him, and not ask questions because we feel he's told us the answer already, or we should know better. It's okay. Don't be concerned your faith isn't strong enough — God knows how strong your faith is, and in fact only he can develop it further. Tell him everything. He's not upset with you. He loves you.

God Has His Own Goals

I forget that God is real. That Jesus is real. I hold onto a thought — "Please God, let *this* happen." As if, if what I want doesn't happen, God has let go of me. As if God's with me less if I don't get a job when I'm unemployed.

But God is real; he's holding me, and he has his own goals. God's goals for me are his own, of his choosing. He may want me to be unemployed for a while. He may want me to move. I can trust in the things he's told me — the eternal things. He'll never leave me nor forsake me (Deuteronomy 31:6). He died for me. I'm valuable to him. Jesus died for me — so he'll never forget me. I matter to him, so much, that he gave up his life for me.

So when I panic over my circumstances, I know that God is still with me, and still in control. I ache over hardship, but God's not with me any less if bad things happen. He hasn't let go, or looked away, or deviated from his plans for me. God's holding onto me, and has an eternal path laid out. I don't need to be afraid. I matter to God. "I will not forget you! See, I have engraved you on the palms of my hands" (Isaiah 49:15–16).

If I'm going through hardship, God is still with me, and will guide me to the right place for him. My entire Christian journey is in Jesus' hands. God loves me, and will protect me, even in death. I need not worry. I'm where God wants me to be. I'm with God. And I always will be, forever.

He Wants to Heal Us

I have come that they may have life, and have it to the full.

— John 10:10

Jesus cares about us so much, he won't "half" take care of our lives. He won't "half" help us. He gave up his life for us — bought our lives with his — so he's profoundly devoted to us. His goal is to heal us completely. He's very serious about our lives, and taking care of us. He sees our whole lives, and has planned great things. He sees every inch of pain, and wishes to heal all of it, thoroughly and completely. He doesn't cast a blind eye over our pain. If we're suffering, he's allowing this only to the measures he decides. He hasn't forgotten our suffering. As if we're far from him, and that's why we're in pain.

    He cares about us, and he cares about others. He has planned great things. He's in complete control. He's with us when we're sad. When we're struggling, or feel guilty and ashamed. We may feel badly, but he's in control of and managing our pain. Our pain is not our fault. Cope with it as best you can. He's with us every moment we ache, and he's in control of our healing — not us alone. He walks with us every step, and will never look away. He has carefully planned our lives, our journey. He loves us. He loves us.

We're Not Trapped

One of the most important things I've learned about Christianity is that what God has promised us is always true, no matter how we feel. We can feel awful, and full of dread, and that God isn't with us. But this doesn't match up with the Bible, or God's true nature. We can feel completely alone, and that we're bound to the things that are wrong with us, or wrong in our life. We can feel guilty and ashamed and trapped. But God has said so many things against this. He'll never leave us (Deuteronomy 31:6). He frees us from sin (John 8:34–36). He'll bear our burdens (Matthew 11:28–30). And he loves us so much, he died for us, to make up for all we do wrong.

It's not about feelings. How we feel is not an indication of how things actually are. It's not as if God doesn't love us, if we don't feel loved. He does. He always has, and always will. The real truth and meaning of life doesn't change based on how we feel. Have faith in this. Give thanks and be grateful, because we have an amazing gift — the gift of God. Remember — be aware. Never forget. The real truths are always true. Our feelings don't change that.

The Real God

God is always far lovelier and sweeter than we think. Our minds are filled with negative images of God — images of judgment, harshness, and of needing to "be good" to please him. We feel inadequate and are very unkind to ourselves, telling ourselves we're not good enough for God. Our hearts ache with pain and loneliness. We feel alone, even with the love of God surrounding us and always being there.

But God, the real God, is kind, gentle, and caring. The barriers we feel between ourselves and God are not caused by him, but by our own thinking. If we saw, even for a second, the depth of his love for us, all of our pain would be wiped away.

In that second, we would see complete acceptance, and a deep, profound love. We would see forgiveness, kindness, and a God who wants to take our burdens from us, and carry us to a place of peace. He wishes to hold us, and calm our fears. He wants to ease our anxiety and take away our pain.

God is always far lovelier and sweeter than we think. He's astonishing. We would feel no pain, if we truly knew him. That's not to say our pain is our fault — God will bring us to a place of healing and understanding in his own timing. But our goal should be to truly know and love God. To be safe in his arms. To be protected. He loves us. We just need to know it.

How Good He Is

God is amazing. He is in control, and his plans can't be altered or stopped by anything. It's not how much we do that gives us protection by God. It's how much he does. We're not safe because we do the right thing or are good people; we're safe because God is protecting us, because we have a relationship with him through Jesus. We can't alter God's plans if we don't do enough, or fall down, or do something wrong. God doesn't let go of us — ever. Our relationship with him remains. He controls our lives and looks after us because of how good he is, not how good we are. As long as we remain with him, he protects us. He'll always protect us. Our lives can be in a bad place, but we're still loved, watched, and cared for by God. He manages every step we take. He holds onto us, and doesn't look away. It's about how good he is. And he's perfect.

Jesus Owns My Life

I always take far too much ownership and responsibility for my life. Jesus owns my life. My life belongs to him. He'll do everything.

I criticize myself for not doing enough, but truthfully I could *never* do enough for God. I criticize myself for not being completely pure of heart, and not caring enough about something, but my heart could *never* be pure enough for God.

God is in control of where I go, what I do, how I feel, what happens to me. If I worked very hard and did a million things right, it would be nothing without Jesus. It's because Jesus stands before me, that God can accept me. What Jesus does with my life is what will bring me closer to God. It's not me alone — it does not rest on my shoulders. God cares that I try, but if I don't try hard enough I won't be breaking a rule and letting God down.

It's not on my shoulders. My path, my journey, my direction, is out of my hands. It's not about meeting a perfect standard, or being "good" enough. I'll never be good enough. Jesus is doing everything — he's controlling my pain, my struggles, my situation. It's he who takes me where I need to be. It's him. I'll never be good enough. I'm loved, and cared for. Jesus owns my life. My life belongs to him.

Nothing Can Separate Us

God understands when we do the wrong thing. He's not ashamed of us.

When I do the wrong thing, like lose my temper and snap at someone, I usually imagine God looking at me and disapproving. I'll think he still loves me, but I'll imagine God standing from afar, wishing I would obey the Bible and behave properly. He's separate from me, and there's a wall of the "righteous" way to behave between us.

But when I see Jesus more clearly, I know this isn't true. Jesus shows me that he understands when I make mistakes — he understands my behavior, and shows me other people can behave that way too. He's not saying it's okay to, for example, lose my temper, but he stands beside me and says, "I know why you did that." He teaches me lovingly that other people can behave that way too, and I shouldn't hate myself and think I'm abnormal.

Jesus is amazing. When we think he'll judge us, he loves us — truly loves us. He longs to show us his love, and teach us to love ourselves. He's not ashamed. He's patient and kind, and sweet and understanding. He doesn't stand from afar in judgment, but sits right next to us, and wants us to be happy. He desires closeness, with no barriers or walls.

Jesus died to take the place for our sin, and bring us close to God. Do we think *anything* we do could break that bond? Could be so bad the sacrifice of God himself would not be enough to make up for it? There's *nothing* that can separate us from God. Nothing we do or don't do. Not our mistakes, not if we don't go to church, not if we're not "godly" enough. There's nothing that can separate us from God. He loves us.

Putting God First

I'm often very hard on myself about putting God first, and not letting my own desires get in the way. About letting God have control, and not deriving happiness from the "wrong" things.

But God isn't upset with us if we don't always put him first, or if we don't think of him properly all the time. He's very patient and forgiving, and will correct us in his own, loving, perfect way.

God is extremely forgiving about us trying to take control. What we need to remember is that he's in control of being in control of us. We don't have to think exactly right or behave exactly right for God to be in control. He just is. We can't take away his control, unless we leave him altogether.

It goes without saying that we'll think and do the wrong thing sometimes. God is forgiving of this. He's so kind and sweet. We can think the wrong thing and be selfish sometimes, and he still totally loves and accepts us.

Don't fear your own mind and heart, as if you'll betray God. He's not that precious. He forgives all. Live, try, and be yourself. Ask for forgiveness when you fall down. It's not about never falling. It's about him lovingly picking us back up.

God Will Carry Us

I usually think I need to have an enormous amount of control in my life. I feel deeply responsible for my life and journey, and feel I have to make careful, thorough steps to ensure I'm following God properly, and doing things properly.

But God has me, and expects far less from me than I do for myself. That's not to say God doesn't care what we do, but *he's* in control — we don't have to do everything right to ensure our lives work out. That's his job. Even if we just barely got out of bed and just barely did some things each day, that's okay. God isn't upset with us if we do things badly, or only just get by.

Our lives working out or heading in a certain direction is based on God's strength, not our own. He wants us to relax and not feel pressured. We just need to make small steps, and God will do the rest. He'll take care of the big picture, and of guiding us. We only need to do things a bit at a time, and day by day.

Don't plan too much and don't stress. God will manage things. He'll make up for what we lack. He'll fill in what we leave out, and carry us to a better place. It's not on us. It's not all on us. It's God's job to manage our lives, and his wish to do this. He loves us, and wants us to relax. He will carry us.

God's Love is Genuine

I sometimes go to a dark place, where I look upon myself as being inherently bad. I think that because of God's concept of being with everyone who turns to Jesus, I'm acceptable to him. But I'm an ugly, black soul, who is only okay because of a concept.

Yes, it's true that God is with us because Jesus died for us. I believe very strongly that God accepts me because of this, not my own merit. However, I turn God's love for me into an obligation on his part, in which he doesn't *like* me but loves me because he has to — he's God and he loves everyone. He loves me only because Jesus died for me.

But God loved me first. God loved me before I became a Christian. He's loved me my whole life. He sees my good qualities — my heart, my soul. He loves me like a parent loves their child, with affection and a genuine concern and compassion for me.

And Jesus? He didn't look at me with disgust, then go through the horror of his death because he had to. He did it for me, out of love. He loves me *so much* that he paid the penalty for what I do wrong, to allow me to be close to God. There's no disgust, or obligation, or anything about rules in Jesus' love for me. He truly loves me.

God likes us. We're treasured. We're smiled upon. Jesus loved us *first*, before his sacrifice. God loved us first, and accepts us without us needing to be perfect, and no matter what we do. God loves us. He likes us.

God Accepts Us

God doesn't care if our prayers aren't perfect. It's easy to think our prayer isn't deep enough, or our heart isn't pure enough when we pray. However, God hears our words, and sees the smallest amount of good intention as being beautiful. He doesn't care if we're not consumed with grief over the other person. He takes our small prayer seriously, and is so pleased we're talking to him.

God doesn't care if our intentions aren't perfect, or we're not trying as hard as we can. Our importance as people isn't based on merit — on how hard we work. God judges people differently from this. He loves us, with a love so pure and strong that nothing on earth can touch it.

There's nothing on earth stronger than God's love. We won't always see this clearly, and often have to take our steps in life with a cloud of confusion hanging over us. God loving us doesn't mean there won't be trials, and pain, and disappointment. But the one thing that we can trust as eternal, the one thing that will always be true, is that God loves us.

He loves us if we do badly — if we fail — if we lose our job or make mistakes in our relationships. His love isn't based on what we do, or feel, or achieve. He just loves us, as we are.

He loves us if we do the wrong thing, or aren't as honorable as those around us say we should be. He loves us if we don't love him, or think of him. He waits for each one of us every day, if we're separate from him.

God takes the small steps we make, and transforms our lives, and the lives of those around us. We only need to make small steps, and he'll carry us the rest of the way. He's pleased with us when we talk with him, and treasures every moment. God accepts us, as we are.

We're Here With a Purpose

God carefully puts us in our position. Even if it's a difficult and scary place. He places us where we are, with a purpose and a reason, and with meticulous planning. God won't let us slip out of his grasp, and have us fall into a bad place he's not in control of. As if by our own error or because we didn't look at him properly, that we ended up where we are.

God is in control of every moment of our lives — every situation, every hardship, every relationship, every interaction, every issue. He sees every single detail, and knows what to do. He'll never give us more than we can handle. We'll be pushed and feel the ache, but God won't let go of us. He knows everything.

We need to go out there and try to find the answer, but God is in control of our journey. We can pray to him about anything, and he'll hear and help us. It may not be how we expect. But he'll help us, and do what's right.

God loves us very dearly, and loves those around us. Do what you can, but don't lose hope, because he'll protect you. We can't say, "I believe in God so *this* will happen." But we can say he loves us and will protect us. Pray for strength. Pray for hope. Pray for love. He hears you.

Be with him out of love

I feel as if I need to look at God exactly right. As if he'll "slip away" if I'm not looking at him properly. I feel I need to have a very strict focus on God, not letting other things shift my view from him. Where I am with God needs to be very *clearly, strictly* placed in my mind. It's not about living my life and turning to God out of a desire for love and nurturing; it's about having a clearly defined focus on him, or I'll be *betraying* him and my entire Christian walk will fall apart. I feel our relationship is a servant-master one, and I'll fail in my duty.

But this isn't right. Jesus is truly loving and accepting of us. There isn't a criterion for interacting with God. It's about love. We can live our lives, and get absorbed in our work and loves. We should be with God because we love him.

I worry I'll start to turn away from God and not love him anymore, but if I hold onto him by the smallest amount, he'll keep a firm grasp on my life. God won't let go of me! He loves me! It's not about structure and rules. It's not about having a clear image of God in my mind. I just need to love him.

Pray. Cry out. Be with God in a natural way. He'll hold onto us. He has a plan for all of us, and he doesn't get distracted from that plan. It's not even up to us to fulfil certain criteria, for God's plans to work. It's about his strength, and his will. God is gracious and forgiving and kind. Be with him out of love. It's why he's with us.

God Gives to Us

God gives to us even though we're completely undeserving.

I usually feel I have to earn God's love. That he loves me because I'm kind. He loves me because I work hard. He loves me because I have a good heart. But if I think this way, it means if I'm unkind, or don't work hard, or have a cold heart, then God doesn't love me.

God doesn't love and accept me because of what I do or feel. God loves me because I'm me, and he accepts me because Jesus died for me, to make up for all I do wrong. God loved me from the moment I existed. But he's able to accept me and give to me because Jesus died for me.

It's terrible when I behave badly or have hatred in my heart, but God isn't with me less because of this. As long as I stay with Jesus, in whatever way I can, God stays with me.

We can't say that if Jesus didn't die for us then God wouldn't love us. He's always loved everyone. But what Jesus has done is so significant, that God will never look away from us. We will do the wrong thing, and deserve to be punished. But Jesus has paid our penalty.

There's no wall between us and God. No standard of behavior to reach. No requirement of us to do the right thing all the time, for us to be with him. All we have to do is ask Jesus to be with us, then stay with him. Ask for forgiveness when we do the wrong thing. What Jesus has done for us wipes out our sin, and we're acceptable and clean. God gives to us even though we're completely undeserving. His love is that great.

We're Not Failing

Jesus wants us to spend time with him, not because he's upset with us for "failing in our duty," but because he loves us and wants to reassure us. He wants to tell us he loves us, warm our hearts, and calm our fears and worries.

Jesus died for us. He doesn't stand over us in judgment, disappointed because we're not living up to a standard. What he gives us will always outweigh what we give him. He wants us to be with him because he loves us. He wants to hold onto us and help us throughout our lives.

Being with Jesus is always about love. Pure, real love, not judgment or harsh rules and standards. Don't fear you're failing God. He doesn't look at you that way.

Only God Can Make Me Love Him

Recently I was plagued by thoughts of God judging me. I was going through a difficult time in my life; then when I became upset with God, I felt he was standing in the distance, frowning upon me and saying I should know better. He's God and he's perfect, and I'm a lowly human who is wrong and foolish.

There seemed to be a great divide between me and God, a divide in which I was struggling to cope with hardship in my life, and all I felt from him was judgment — he wanting me to have perfect faith, and not sympathizing with me at all. Usually I feel God crossing the divide between us with great love and acceptance, acceptance enabled by the loving act of Jesus' sacrifice; but this all seemed to disappear because of my feelings of rejection and admonishment by God.

I now feel close to God again, but not because my situation improved. Despite my anger and despair with God, Jesus came to me and said he's not judging me. He said he accepts me; his sacrifice breaks down all walls, and any burden on me to do the right thing or have a strong faith to be with him is obliterated. He eased the pain and rejection I felt, and held me close. He looked at me with love.

I realized Jesus' love is stronger than all my worries, anxiety and fear. Most of all, I realized it's not up to me to believe in God perfectly, or even have a deep love for him, for our relationship to last. God controls our relationship lasting. He holds onto me. Only he can give me a heart that can love him. My feeble, doubting heart, is not the measure of my relationship with God. It's God's strong, powerful heart. His love. His love.

The experience I went through was difficult and painful. There will always be pain in our Christian walk. But I know

God loves me, strongly and truly. I know he'll rescue me. I know he's in control of all I go through. I pray he brings me peace.

It's God's Job to Change Me

God is in control. I feel inadequate and jealous of others, as if I'm behind and worse than other people. I feel as if I desperately need to catch up to others. But God holds me and says he'll carry me to where I need to be. I don't need to struggle and strive and feel ashamed of where I am. It's not on my shoulders to transform myself, as God will change me, in his time and in his way. It's not my fault I haven't reached a further point in my life. *It's not my fault* — it's God's job to change me.

God will make me love him. God will enable me to understand him. God will develop my faith, and heal my heart. *I don't need to feel so responsible.* It's not as if, if I don't feel love for God, then God isn't with me and our relationship halts. My relationship with God is controlled by him, and his unwavering love for me.

I can fall apart and be weak; feel anger and hatred toward God and others. God still loves me, and is still in control of healing and changing me. I can only be real with God. Be honest. If I feel anger or fear; hatred or worry, God knows already. I can't pretend to be someone I'm not. I can only be myself.

God is in control of my life. Of changing me, and my emotions. Of what I need to do and where I need to go. Of my responsibilities toward others. God will control it all, and enable me to be who I'm meant to be. I don't need to go to a place deep inside to find an inner strength. God is my strength. Just hold onto Jesus, by the smallest amount. Feel weak and frail and worried, as you can only feel how you feel. God is your strength. He'll rescue you and make you strong. Just be yourself. It's all you can be.

GOD EASES THE PRESSURE WE FEEL

I'm going through my day, trying to complete my tasks and feeling a great deal of pressure. I'm trying to be responsible and ethical and hard working, and am very concerned about doing things properly.

Then I feel for a moment what God is like. God doesn't place this pressure on me. He wants me to be calm and to relax. He wishes to bear my burdens. I don't have to worry about doing things perfectly to succeed — whether I succeed or not is based on God's strength, and his wishes and desires. God looks at me with such love, and tells me to calm down and not to worry. I'm not on my own, with my problems and my situation. I'm with God.

Even if I'm overwhelmed with a dark situation, and feel as if I'm doing the wrong thing — God doesn't reject me because of this. He's still with me, *with me in the situation*, and offering his love just as much as if nothing were wrong. He loves us. His love isn't conditional on us doing the right thing. His love is eternal and bound to us.

We can breathe easier. We don't need to be stressed. God has us. He'll protect us. He'll manage all our situations. He'll control what will happen. If we ask for forgiveness, God wipes our slate clean. He loves us so strongly. He has us, and will control our lives.

God Sees Our Pain

God smiles upon me and understands all I go through — all the things that trouble me, and all the stresses I feel. He doesn't frown upon me for being upset, or frustrated. He doesn't look at my dark thoughts and judge me, but instead completely understands where I'm coming from.

God doesn't see a dark thought and label us as "racist," but instead sees the pain behind that thought — every experience, every hardship, every difficulty. He understands what we're going through. God in no way supports racism, but he won't stand over us and judge us for having difficulty with a multicultural situation.

Only acceptance brings about healing. We won't learn to love others, unless we feel loved and accepted ourselves. Only God being next to us, saying he loves us, can heal the dark part of our hearts, which judges and despises. It's not about us being "good" — never having a dark thought, or never feeling hatred or acting badly. It's about realizing we're totally loved and accepted, as we are, and our every thought and feeling originates from somewhere understandable. We're not broken. We're normal.

God sees us, and will heal every dark part of us. Don't hate yourself, for feeling how you feel. For judging how you judge. Sometimes we'll be wrong, and the person before us will be doing nothing wrong. But at all times, God sees our heart, and knows the pain that brought us to where we are now. It's not about not feeling how we feel, and never making a mistake. It's about realizing God totally loves and accepts us, then we can be complete and healed and whole. It's all about God's love. It always was.

God Will Help Us

I often think that God helps me based on my level of faith, and how close I am to him. How much I obey him. I think he helps me based on where I am in my relationship with him.

But God helps me because of how good Jesus is. Jesus has bought my life; paid for my sins with his death. My life is owned by him. When God sees me, he sees Jesus standing before me, wiping out all my sins and carrying me through my life. Making up for everything I lack, and everything I can't do. God sees Jesus before me when he looks at me, so any plans he has for my life are based on how good *Jesus* is, not how good I am.

God plans great things for me and blesses me; he answers my prayers and eases my pain. He is gracious to me and forgiving; he carries me through my troubles and heals me. He loves me — always has — but he helps me based on how good Jesus is.

So when I'm praying for God to help me or a loved one, I needn't feel guilty or ashamed or unworthy. I'll always be unworthy. But God sees Jesus before me, blotting out my sins and shame, and helps me because my debt is paid. God *will* help me because he loves me, and *can* help me because I'm washed clean.

It's not how strongly I believe in God which will lead him to help me, or if I'm a good person; have behaved well recently or spent hours praying. Whether my mind and heart have been clean. I'm flawed. Always will be. But Jesus is perfect, and he *died* for me. Nothing can take that away. So God can, and will, help me. No matter how sinful I am.

When God Is Quiet

We go about our lives and measure it by our successes — the big things we can point to that make us who we are. We feel we need a constant stream of important moments in our lives, otherwise we aren't succeeding. Our lives aren't amounting to much. We're failing.

Our lives can have just as much meaning, and be progressing exactly how they're meant to, in the quiet times. The quiet times that build patience, that stretch our being, that give us time to grow and mend from the prior times of adversity. Life is hard, and difficult, and painful; we only make it harder on ourselves if we feel we must be constantly succeeding, when it can be a blessing to not be suffering. We have high standards for ourselves. Patience means so much, and the quiet doesn't mean we're failing.

The thing to remember in our quiet is that God plans every moment of our lives — the good, the bad, the rest. I can feel if I'm not getting words from God — if I'm not feeling his presence on a daily basis — that I'm far from him. That I need to be more diligent and work harder to be closer to him. Sometimes this may be true. But God isn't with me any less when I don't sense him strongly. God gives me so much when I don't even ask for it, and haven't earned a single thing. Do I think that, when I'm not hearing from him, that he's disowned me? That I'm not doing enough for him? Does God love me less?

Of course not! If he loves me without me deserving it at one time, this applies at all times. God isn't with me less if I don't hear from him. He's perfectly capable of acting in my life, and doesn't need permission from me to bend my life to his will. He'll do that, regardless of how "good" I am. God's truths hold firm, no matter what we're going through, even if what we're going through is the monotony of everyday life. Be grateful for the quiet. It's God giving us a rest, and exactly what we need at the time. He loves us. Nothing can change that.

GOD ON OUR SIDE

Commit your way to the Lord;
trust in him and he will do this:
he will make your righteous reward shine like the dawn,
your vindication like the noonday sun.

Be still before the Lord
and wait patiently for him;
do not fret when people succeed in their ways,
when they carry out their wicked schemes.

— Psalm 37:5–7 TNIV

I get so frustrated when people treat me unfairly. I become completely heartbroken, anxious and upset. I worry for my pain, and, if someone I love is hurting me, I'm distraught for them — concerned for their happiness and their heartache. It's some of the worst kind of pain.

God has given me hope over this situation from the above psalm. God will always protect those who are with him, and see that we receive the best that we deserve in the end. People will treat me badly and be completely unfair, but God will always stand by me. God will *always* stand by me. God is totally, wholeheartedly, completely on my side, at all times. He always sees my point of view. Always sees my side. Always sees my heart. He's just as offended when I'm treated unfairly as anyone who loves me would be. He completely cares for me, and my welfare.

God will always stand by me. With God on my side how can I lose? How can I really lose, in the end? God sees the good in my heart and soul, and has told me I'm okay as I am.

He loves me. He'll support me, and ensure that things will work out.

Being treated unfairly can cause so much pain, but we need to believe in God, not that the situation will be rectified because of something we do to control things. God will fix things. We don't know what will happen, but in the end God will look after us.

I try to look at things in too grand a manner sometimes, and wonder how God can be on my side, and on the side of every other Christian at once. But I don't need to think this way. This kind of thinking stems from insecurity. I just need to be present with God, with him in the moment, and trust the things he says to me. If God says he'll protect me, then he will. If God says I'm okay as I am, then I am, no matter what anyone says. God loves us. He's on our side.

God is My Strength

Throughout my life I have faltered and become distressed, feeling insecure over my mistakes. My inner strength has been weakened when people tell me I'm not good enough. I've become very sad and hurt, and felt all alone. I have so much negative self-talk, and have felt small and unloved.

But now, very slowly, I'm developing a stronger inner self; where who I am is not about me, and whether I do everything right. It's about who God is.

God is my backbone and who I lean on. God is my heart and my soul. God reassures me and comforts me, and, even when I feel terrible, I know God hasn't changed and still loves me. God is always with me, and my core is strengthened by his unchanging, magnificent self.

I'm not alone. I'm not alone, with my insecurity and my negative thoughts. God stands next to me and holds me up — he holds onto me, and says I'm alright. God holds my head up, straightening me and making me look ahead, not down in misery. Jesus is with me. He's my heart, and my life.

So much can change in our lives: our circumstances, the way people treat us, our health, and even our feelings can constantly change. But God will *never* change. He's the one thing that is forever constant, forever the same, and we can hold firm to him. He controls everything that happens — has controlled *everything* that has *ever* happened, and nothing is out of his hands. Nothing will escape him, or ever be missed by him. He sees everything.

When we feel hurt; when we're inundated with trial after trial, God is there. He's there even if we're angry at him. He's there even if we blame him. He's there at all times, in every moment, and we need not feel alone or afraid.

Life can hurt, so much, but Jesus sees all of our pain. He died to obliterate every bad thing from the world. His pain heals our own. His suffering takes ours away. Our pain is designed to bring us a greater joy, and Jesus is the source of that joy.

God is my strength. I'm becoming who I'm meant to be because of him. I can't do it on my own. I can't change on my own. God is my core, and my center. He'll keep me strong. He'll keep me safe.

Taking Care of Others

God is sympathetic with us. Sometimes in our lives we have to take care of another person long term, whether they are elderly or seriously ill. We take on the enormous responsibility for looking after someone, and all the self sacrifice this entails. It can be very hard work, and we need to be constantly available and focused on the other person. One of the most difficult aspects of this is the emotional burden we feel.

As Christians, we can unfortunately think of God as standing over us, commanding we love others and be completely selfless at all times. We expect if we fall short of that, then he'll be disappointed in us.

God does value love and giving, but he's entirely understanding of us, and knows the burden we feel when we look after others. He knows that caring for another person is difficult, and we're going to feel upset, hurt and weary.

Thoughts of wanting to be alone sometimes, and wanting our old lives back; of wishing we could just *rest* and enjoy all life has to offer — God understands these thoughts. He doesn't think badly of us for thinking this way. God understands our need to be selfish sometimes — needing to have our own identity, and not have our entire life be about caring for another person. We're doing something tough, exhausting and selfless, and can often feel stretched to our limit and worn out.

Jesus feels our pain. And he'll give us rest. He'll reward us for our hard work. God sees it as the ultimate act of beauty and love to sacrifice our life to look after another, but we can't tell ourselves we shouldn't find this difficult. Of course we will. Christ stands by our side, helping us, and he'll reward us for our hard work. Hold fast to him, and have faith that your life is where it should be. Not just for the person you're caring for, but for you. God cares for your life, and has great plans for you. Your heart will be eased. You are, and always will be, loved.

Feeling Guilty Over Our Focus

I was working hard redesigning my website — spending a great deal of time transferring my work and refining everything — but was filled with a huge sense of guilt. Even though my website is about God, and the point of my words is to bring people closer to him, I kept hearing a voice inside me saying: "You're not spending enough time with God. You're ignoring him. You have an obligation to spend a lot of time with God, and feel whole and centered with him. If you don't feel close to him, you're doing something wrong."

This is a dilemma we often face. I've read countless words, people saying what we really care about is what we're spending time on. Admonishing us for living, for working, for experiencing life, if our heart isn't totally focused on God at all times. Our heart, our soul, and our center, need to be always in the "right" place. We can't just be ordinary people, who work hard, and are focused on what we're doing. We have a duty to fulfil. God will be disappointed in us.

The guilt we feel for not always focusing on God isn't from him. God isn't upset with us for working hard. He looks at us with love, and is pleased we're trying to be responsible. God doesn't stand over us and think: "You don't love me enough. You're not thinking of me and looking at me enough."

God says: "I love you. I'll always be here for you. I want you to know I accept you as you are, and don't think badly of you. I can see into your heart and soul, and my only desire is to heal and help you. When you're working, I'm with you, holding onto you, even if you can't see me. I'm with you every step you take. My only desire is to love and care for you. I died for you, so you would never have to suffer alone. I'm with you. I'm proud of you. Be with me out of love, not out of feeling forced or guilty. I love you, and will always wait for you. I'm always with you."

God loves us. Remember that, not the guilt. God doesn't give us guilt — it's not from him. He covers us with love. When people go to Jesus in the first place, it's about his love, and promise to heal and help us. If we go to God because of his love for us, then guilt is not what should keep us with him. Be with him out of love. He'll always hold onto us. No matter what we're doing.

God is Only About Love

When I'm reading about God, I often become very sad and upset. While there's some good information out there, a lot of the time Christians write about God with an air of what we "should" do; the things we ought to do, the way we ought to think, the ways we're failing God.

The attitude seems to be that God loves us, but we must turn away from how we live our lives — give up who we are, and everything we know. We must be completely different, always being vigilant, constantly remembering God and his words, or we'll turn away from him. We have to wash ourselves clean of who we are, or we'll get lost in a sinful life.

It's heartbreaking that this seems to be the attitude often projected onto Christians and non Christians alike, to represent our relationship with God. It's not true. None of it.

Jesus is completely loving. You could spend a thousand years dwelling on his love, and still not comprehend the majesty of it all. He loves us, more than the most loving, kind, accepting person ever could. *More.* He accepts us at all times. When we do the wrong thing. When we feel ashamed of ourselves. When we've acted out in pain and frustration. He's the kind voice in our heart, telling us he understands why we did what we did, and holding us in his arms.

He's with us if we hate him. If we're mad at him. If we blame him for how hard our lives are. He's with us every moment, comforting us and telling us we're alright. Even if it takes years to hear him, he's there. He's always been there. He'll always be there.

We don't need to change our lives so Jesus can accept us. Jesus accepts us, so we can change our lives. If we need to. He'll always love and accept us. He bore our sins on the cross, not because he thinks we're awful, but so we can be accepted by God, without ever being punished for our faults and our mistakes. It's all about love.

So don't listen when people say you're not good enough as you are, and need to turn your life upside down to be with God. God's already turned the world upside down, to be with you. He's all about love, and that's the only message you need to know about him. Spend your time being immersed in words of his love, as a true knowledge of God's love is all you'll ever need to stay with him. Not giving up your life, or forcing yourself to behave a certain way. Be you. Feel how you feel. Tell God how you feel. Tell God everything. He knows already. And he's waiting for you.

The Loveliness of God

Jesus is very kind and sweet. He's not angry with us, when we're angry with him. He doesn't expect from us, the huge amount we expect from ourselves. He'll bear our burdens. Truly. He'll take away our pain. If it takes a long time, it's not because we're not doing enough. It's all part of his plan.

We truly need to do very little in our relationship with God. We need to stay with him, and try; but Jesus does almost everything. Even if we're upset with God, if we just stay with him, Jesus will bring us closer to him. It's not entirely up to us to heal our relationship with God. Jesus will do that.

When we feel overwhelmed in our troubles, and feel ashamed of our mistakes — God doesn't see us this way. It's not up to us to behave perfectly, for Jesus to rescue us from the things that trouble us. From the bad situation we're in. We don't have to "earn" his help. He'll help us anyway, no matter what we've done, because he loves us. Jesus doesn't hold us accountable, the way we hold ourselves accountable. His love is pure, and real, and strong. He doesn't blame us. He'll help us out of love, not because we've met certain criteria, or behaved well.

Jesus is very kind, and sweet. He's beautiful and lovely. He's God. He loves us, and always will.

We Don't Have a Divine Duty

We think of God as being separate from us, only concerned with the higher purpose of saving people, and having people evangelize about him. He's up in heaven, dealing with life and death, and as Christians we need to be perpetually worried about life and death too. It's all about the mission. We have a mission to fulfil.

But God cares about our daily lives, and our work and loves, the way we do. We think of him as being extremely serious, but God cares about our happiness, not how we can save the world for him.

God cares about how we're doing at school and work. He cares about the projects we're undertaking. He cares about our relationships with our friends, and when we're in love. He's with us in every detail of our lives, and he sees those details as precious.

We get absorbed in our projects and feel guilty, as if we're doing the wrong thing by not focusing on God. But God's pleased we're working on something. Just like a loving parent, he wants to see us do well, and is happy we're using our gifts. He's so happy we're working hard, and making something of our lives. He's invested in us doing well, because he wants us to be happy and satisfied. He doesn't frown upon us if we're not working on something to do with Christianity.

We need to stop thinking of God's relationship with us as one of obligation, in which we have a part to play, and a fixed, religious duty to fulfil. It's not like that. Our relationship with God is an individual one, between us and him. We only need to focus on loving him, and receiving his love. Trying to love him in our own, personal way.

If God has a job for us to do, he'll lead our lives in the direction to do it. It's not about us placing pressure on ourselves, to fulfil a "divine duty." Ignore that pressure. Just focus on an intimate, personal relationship with God. Hold onto his love tightly, to get you through your life. Lean on him. Talk to him. Cry out. He cares about you, and every minute aspect of your life. He loves you if you never perform any "Christianly" duties for him. He loves you for you, as you are.

When We're Lonely

When I become very lonely, my first thought is that people will criticize me. I imagine even God will criticize me, telling me I'm not being sociable enough, and I brought this on myself. I imagine God will tell me I need to meet a suitable standard of being with people, or else I'm not good enough as a person. I need to go out there and make friends, or else I'm lacking and not doing what I should.

God doesn't speak to us this way. He accepts me as I am. He smiles upon me, and reminds me that he completely, totally loves me, and would give up anything for me. He spends every moment of every day with me, and is by my side in everything I go through. He's always with me. I may become very lonely at times, but God doesn't stand over me and judge me, telling me I'm a loser and not good enough. He loves me.

God reminds me his love is all the love I'll ever need. Only a cold, harsh person would criticize someone for being lonely, and put pressure on them to be different, saying they're not good enough. God says he loves us, we're good enough as we are, and we're not alone. He's with us. We'll never be alone again, while he's with us. He'll help us grow. He'll help us become happier.

Feeling lonely doesn't mean we're alone. We have someone by our side, who holds onto us, and cares about every aspect of our lives. God forgives every bad thing we do, and reminds us of the goodness inside of us. We'll never be alone again. We're loved. We're watched over. We're cared for. We're safe.

We Belong Here

As Christians, we're often told we need to be separate from everyone else. We need to live as if we don't belong here. We are not of this world.

But Jesus created this world. God created it, and sent Jesus to reclaim the earth and all of its people for him. As Christians we *are* of this world — we live here with Christ, in a relationship with God.

Being a Christian doesn't mean living separately from everyone else; it just means enjoying life the way it was meant to be. Enjoying life by having a loving relationship with God, and going through everything with him by our side. We're allowed to be happy, and free.

Life can be extremely difficult, and Christians face the same trials and pain as anyone else. But we tell ourselves we should expect more. There *is* a difficulty in being a Christian — the difficulty of trying to understand God, and trying to live our lives with him. But this is the same difficulty as with anything we do that's worthwhile and meaningful. Being a Christian can be hard, but we make things worse by thinking we can't fully enjoy our lives, and need to suffer.

There will be times of pain. But God will control them. We don't have to think about pain, as if we should expect more of it, and almost be joyous when we're suffering. I'm not joyous when I'm suffering. I'm miserable. I get through tough times by trying to be strong, and remembering God's still with me, even if I don't understand him and hate everything in my life at that moment. I just try to be myself, and get through things any way I can.

God doesn't expect more of us because we're Christians. God doesn't expect from us, anywhere near what we expect from ourselves. God loves us. He wants us to be happy, and enjoy life. Things will be difficult sometimes. There will be times of pain. But this applies to everyone. We don't need to be separate from the world. We just need to be.

We're Doing What We Can

God once told me it wasn't my fault — my guilt, my isolation, the other ways I turned out. He said I've done what I could with what I had.

When I was a kid, I didn't do anything special. I wasn't doing brilliantly at school or making a special effort to make friends, or going to therapy to deal with the negativity in my life. I was just me. I didn't think perfectly, deflecting all negative thoughts, so the darkness wouldn't get to me. In fact, the darkness did get to me. Severely. I just lived, barely got by, and coped badly. It was a mess. It was all a dark, horrible mess, and I was incredibly scarred.

I have a lot of problems, as an adult. I constantly feel I'm a bad person. I can become quite isolated, and withdraw from life. I've struggled with depression for many years, and carry a huge layer of guilt with me at all times.

But God said it wasn't my fault. How I turned out. He said I did what I could with what I had. He didn't look over my past and say I should have worked harder to get rid of my negative thoughts, and should have made more friends. He didn't blame me at all, for how I turned out.

In my life now, I feel I need to think and act perfectly. I'm not allowed to be sad — I need to manage my negative thinking, so I don't get depressed. I'm not allowed to be alone — I need to have people around me so I can think correctly and more positively, and not be in my own world. I have to work hard, doing everything correctly, and meeting the right standards. I *can't* let myself down in *any* way, or the negative consequences are my fault.

But God doesn't think this way. Imagine if he'd thought that way about how I grew up. God looks at me and says: however I'm coping, however I'm feeling, however I'm doing, it's okay. It's not my fault. The same rules apply now as when I was a kid, when I wasn't coping and it all fell down around me. I did what I could with what I had. Right now, I'm doing what I can. If I'm upset, lonely, overwhelmed, feeling negative, or even getting depressed, I'm doing what I can. I'm doing what I can, because *however* I'm doing is okay. I'm okay, no matter how I'm doing, because I'm okay as I am.

It's not about meeting a standard. It's about being ourselves. We're okay if we have no friends and are confused and scared and doing the wrong thing; if our lives are falling apart and we're depressed. We're okay, as we are. God doesn't frown upon us and say we're only doing okay if we're coping well. He loves and accepts us as we are, and will never leave us. We don't need to think and act perfectly. We don't need to be coping. We don't need to be happy. We just need to be ourselves. We're doing what we can. God doesn't ask any more of us. He loves us, as we are.

God's Promises of Love

BOOK 2

*E*VEN IF I DO SOMETHING WRONG, ON PURPOSE

I keep thinking there's a standard of behavior I must reach. Now that I'm a more mature Christian, and I write about God, I must be a super Christian who does everything right. It's all about rules and standards.

But God accepts me as I am. Even if I make a million mistakes. Even if I do something wrong, on purpose. I keep thinking that God won't love me unless I'm completely pure inside — completely pure of heart, and everything I do comes from the right place. If I did the wrong thing, I meant well.

But God loves me, even if my heart is black. He loves me. He won't accept me only if I do the right thing, or mean well, or have a pure heart. He accepts me no matter what I do. He truly loves me. It's okay if I'm a mess. It's okay if I make mistakes. It's okay if I do the wrong thing sometimes. God won't accept me only if I make the right choices. He loves me, no matter what I do.

God loves us as if we're children, and wants to hold onto us and protect us as if we're his children. He doesn't have the high expectations of us, that we have of ourselves. He wants us to be calm. He wants us to relax. Don't push yourself too hard. It's okay. God loves us.

We Don't Need to Have Perfect Faith

There are times when God promises me something. I'll feel quite strongly he's saying he'll take care of a certain matter, for example how I'll pay for future expenses. I'll feel that God is carefully managing my life, and, whilst my life will still be a struggle, it will be a struggle under his control. I'm not on my own, and don't have to worry about how I'll afford everything, or get by. God will supply things. He'll help me get by. He'll take care of me.

There's a problem with this scenario, though. When God promises me he'll take care of something, I feel I need to have *perfect* faith — it's an enormous sin to doubt or try to plan for things myself. It's a betrayal to God if I try to budget, or manage things on my own. If I try to "take over." I need to be perfectly still, and allow God to work, or I've failed him. He'll be disappointed and angry with me.

But God doesn't look at me this way. He wants me to have faith that he'll provide for me, because he doesn't want me to worry — it's not that he'll punish me if I don't believe in him. It's not about demonstrating a strong, pure faith, and being "dutiful" — God wants to provide for me because he loves me. He won't punish me if I doubt him, or try to provide for myself.

We only need to be ourselves, and do what we think is right. God won't be angry with us. We can't ruin any plans he has for us. His plans are controlled by him, and will work out the way he intends. The only thing we can do against God is leave him altogether. As long as we stay with him, he forgives and controls everything in our lives. God loves us. God manages our faith in him. Don't blame yourself for doubting. God loves us, as we are.

God Is Always With Us

I forget God manages my life. I keep thinking he's only in charge if I think of him properly — as if his control is bound to how well I behave. That doesn't make sense. Control isn't control if we have to behave perfectly, or God's unable to act. As if God's power is reliant on our behavior.

I'll work hard and get a lot done, then when I rest I'll think, "Okay, God, take over." He was in control the whole time. He managed my highs and lows. My stresses and deep anguish. The problems that tortured me, and the painful paths I had to walk.

I feel I fail constantly, and if only I were closer to God, or looked at him better, then I wouldn't be in pain. I wouldn't be suffering. But God's in control of our suffering. It's not as if we were "stupid" or "wrong," and that's why the path we traveled was so painful.

God is with us when we're failing. When we're in turmoil. When we feel confused and lost and alone — when we feel everyone hates us. God is with us when we feel badly. It's okay to feel awful. It doesn't mean we're doing anything wrong.

God's control isn't measured by if we feel "connected" to him. He just is in control. He makes a promise to take over and heal our lives when we become a Christian, and he'll do that. But the difficult part is we'll still suffer, in order to be led to greater healing. We'll still suffer, so we can learn something we can teach others.

It's not how much we do that determines God's presence in our lives. He's always there, and always active. All we need to do is not blame ourselves when things go wrong, and not hate ourselves for our mistakes. Try and stay with God, even when everything seems hopeless and miserable. He has a higher purpose for us. A plan. He doesn't leave us alone. He doesn't leave us at all. God's in control. He's always with us.

We Can Be Weak

We don't have to do an exact "right" thing. As if there's a rule, or a principle, or a standard to reach. We only need to be ourselves. If something seems horrible and too difficult, we don't have to do it.

I expect God to be standing over me, saying, "Be good." As if, God couldn't bear to be with me if I wasn't trying as hard as I could, or my intentions weren't perfect. As if it's a deep, deep sin not to be "good." Not to be presentable and moral and innocent.

I keep thinking I can't just be myself, with my weaknesses, and be fallible and ordinary. I can't just be myself, and *make mistakes*. God wouldn't dare accept me if I were less than I should be.

But it's not like that. God made us, and he knows we're weak. He sees our sins. He *sees* them, and is still with us, no matter what we do. God loves us, and doesn't look away. There's no exact way to behave, exact way to live. We just need to try, and do what we can. God is our parent, so he accepts our faults, and helps us through our lives. Life is difficult, and messy, but we just need to try. God is with us. He loves us. He'll always be with us, no matter what we do, or how weak we are.

God Doesn't Judge Us

I've felt for years that God is disappointed in me. I feel God has rules and principles, about everything, even my daily tasks. He's watching over me, with a strict objective of how I should behave. Even in his love, there's disapproval.

But God isn't like this. If we think of Jesus as someone who truly loves us, to the point that he would die for each and every one of us; that he loves us *so much* he would be killed, even though he was blameless — then things are different.

Jesus died for me. Me. Would he really stand next to me and say the following? "You're not working hard enough. You didn't write that properly. I expect you to write more often, and perfectly, and not let me down. I have an expectation of you. You owe me this."

Jesus doesn't talk to us this way. It's the expectation we have of ourselves, and what others tell us, that makes us think God judges us. He doesn't. If we were barely getting by, not trying very hard, not doing all we could — Jesus would still love us. He *wants* to carry us. He wants to take care of our lives.

Jesus doesn't become angry with us for not "giving" ourselves enough to him. He won't be upset with us for not surrendering to him enough. He just loves us. No rules. No expectations. No standards. No judgment. He loves us, individually, and is so proud of us.

We find it hard to understand Jesus' love, because it's perfect. No human could love us this way. If only we could truly see God's love. We would be healed. We would be saved. We would be calm. We would be at peace.

Jesus truly loves us. He's working in our lives, even if all we feel is pain, and we don't understand him. He loves us, and doesn't judge. God isn't upset with us if we fail. He's with us, if we ask him to be. And that's all we need do.

We're Not on Our Own

God knows everything that happens in our lives. There's nothing we can do that will make him turn away from us. We can't surprise him or disappoint him. He created us. He knows our thoughts before we think them. He knows everything we do. Everything we've done, or will do. He's not surprised by us, or unprepared for what happens in our lives.

God doesn't have high expectations of us, wanting us to do more or think perfectly. He's not upset if our thinking is confused, or we're constantly anxious and worried. It's normal to worry. It's normal, and God isn't disappointed in us.

It's God's power that enables us to do what we're meant to do. We're not on our own with our work, relying entirely on our strength. It's not our strength at all. God will enable us to do what we're meant to do. It's his strength, and his will. We're not on our own, even if we feel alone and are filled with anxiety. God's carrying us, and is in control of our lives.

We can be at rest. If we worry, it's God that will ease our concerns. If we're upset, it's God that will warm our hearts. If we doubt him, it's God that will give us more faith. We're not on our own. We're not supposed to do everything on our own. We can be calm, and relax. But it's okay if we're upset. God will take care of us, and make us feel better. Do what you can to get through your life. You're not alone.

What God Has Done With His Love

My heart aches, and I'm dragged down by the pain of my life. The trials, the troubles, the problems. Stress gets me down. Failure gets me down. I'm not good enough. I'm not doing enough.

I wonder what can make up for everything that's wrong in my life. For everything I do wrong, and everything I can't do. I wonder what could possibly heal my years of pain, and make up for all the bad things that have happened to me. I'm a failure, as a person. I've been left behind. I'm no one.

It's all well and good to say God loves us, but that doesn't make up for the pain. That doesn't take away the years of scarring. I'm still a failure. Someone loving me doesn't make it so the bad things never happened. Doesn't give me amazing strength, to overcome what I can't do. I still can't do anything. I'm still no one.

But Jesus doesn't just offer love. Love is, of itself, astonishing, but he doesn't just offer love. That wouldn't be enough.

Jesus says: "I've died for everyone's sins. I've paid for the sins of the person that hurt you. The parent that abused you. I've died for their sins — died as punishment, because what they did was so wrong. Someone has been blamed for the scars you bear. I've paid for them. Your scars aren't disregarded. I've shed blood for the sins against you.

"And I've shed blood for your sins. For everything you do wrong, and everything you can't do. I've taken on the burden of your life, and all of your trials. I've taken on the difficulties, the stress, and the weight of what goes wrong in your life. I'm your center. When someone hates you, I feel it. When someone wrongs you, I suffer. I'm your very core, because I died for you, and now your life is owned by me.

"I've paid for every bad thing that has happened to you, and that will happen. I've obliterated those sins. And I've destroyed yours. You're not alone anymore. There's nothing you can do that will make me leave you. Nothing can separate you from me. We'll always be together. I've paid for every bad thing you've done, and will do. And I've paid for all of the sins of the world. I'm in control of it all. You need to remember that, even when you're in pain. I'm always with you. And there's no pain I can't handle."

It takes Jesus' blood to take away our pain. Love isn't enough. Love doesn't make up for the sins of the world. It's what Jesus has *done*, because of his love. I wouldn't be with God if he were an inactive God. If he loved, but took no action to heal the world. I'm with him because he's active, and is doing something for my life and pain. I'm with him because he heals me. Because he offers answers. Because he's real.

God's love *is* enough. Because of what he's done with it.

GOD IS WITH US, EVEN IF WE FEEL BADLY

Our lives can be difficult, dragging us down and making us feel weary. We can feel trapped by sadness and pain, and become so upset. Things can be awful. Life can be so hard.

At these times, I think, *I'm sad because I'm not close enough to God. I should read more about him. Dwell on him more. Pray more. I'm sad because I'm letting Jesus down. It's my fault. Jesus isn't saving me because I'm not doing enough for him.*

Jesus wouldn't be a very good savior, if we had to save ourselves. If he could only heal us if we were doing the right thing. If he could only take away our misery, if our mind and heart were in the right place.

A true savior *saves* — rescues us, when our life is a disaster. Helps us up, when we can't lift ourselves. Jesus doesn't come into our lives, then only act if we've "proved" ourselves.

Jesus comes into our lives, *as they are*, and dwells within us. He experiences everything we do, and offers love, and truth, and peace. He holds onto us closely, and never looks away. He's always with us.

The difficulty is, we won't always feel God's love. In fact, we may rarely feel it at all. Jesus' love for us, and his work in our lives, isn't measured by how good we feel. Just because we feel badly, doesn't mean Jesus isn't at work, or that we're not doing enough for God. Sometimes, we'll feel badly. Sometimes, we'll feel badly for a long time.

Our pain isn't a sign that God is absent, or that he's disappointed in us. He's not standing back, waiting for us to "behave better," before he can act. He's not standing back at all. He's with us from the moment we ask him to be, and never leaves.

God is with us, even if we feel badly. He's always at work in our lives. We'll be sad sometimes, and go through struggles and tough times. It doesn't mean we're alone, or haven't matched up to how we should behave. There's no exact way to behave. Just be yourself, and speak to God as if he's your best friend. God is with us, even if we feel badly.

JESUS CONTROLS OUR PAIN

Jesus experiences everything we do. He feels what we feel. Goes through what we go through. Suffers what we suffer. He lives within us, and experiences all of our trials. Our pain is his. Our problems are his own.

When something horrible is happening to us, we wonder if God will help. The exact same problem is happening to Jesus. He'll take care of the outcome. He won't let the situation go by, without managing what will happen. Let the bad situation occur, until the problem is beyond what we can handle. Jesus will never give us more than we can handle. We can rest. Jesus won't let the bad things go by unchecked. He won't let things become out of control.

Our lives will be awful sometimes, and we'll suffer. But there will be an end point. There will be a limit. It may be beyond what we think is fair. We may think God should have stopped the pain sooner. But he's in control, and knows exactly what he's doing. He only has our best interests at heart. The pain we go through has a higher purpose, and a higher meaning. God doesn't let things happen by accident. He doesn't let things happen without being in control of them.

Jesus experiences everything we do. He's just as upset about our loved one being sick, as we are. He's more upset. He's more distraught over the pain of the world than we'll ever be, and is completely aware of the dark things in our lives. The dark things in the lives of those around us. He's completely aware of the problems of the world, and knows how to fix them. He'll give us work to do, and help us to cope with these things. He won't burden us too strongly.

We don't need to worry about how to fix our problems. Jesus will. We don't need to worry about what we should do to help those we love. Jesus will tell us. He loves us, and those around us. Nothing is out of his control. Jesus controls our pain.

Comfort When We Fail

I try to find happiness in my failures by looking at measurable things. For example, looking at what I'm doing right, or telling myself people like what I do. This isn't wrong, in itself. But I should try to find my happiness in God.

God loves me, and he'll stand by me no matter what. He loves me despite my failures. Jesus loves me even if I make a lot of mistakes. He has a plan for my life. He won't let go, or look away if I do things incorrectly. He loves me as I am.

I should derive comfort from this, instead of looking at myself and what I do right. I'll only feel empty inside, if I try to find my happiness in my own strength and abilities. I fail all the time, and even when I succeed, doing well at something isn't where true happiness comes from. True happiness comes from within — from being loved, and feeling love inside of us. From knowing that God loves us, no matter what we do, or who we are.

Even if we lose our job or fail at our business venture, God stands by us. He has a plan for us. God has a path laid out, and he'll lead us down that path. We don't have to do everything perfectly, or behave exactly right. Say and do all the right things. We just need to be ourselves, and try.

We'll fail, sometimes. But God won't let go of us. Everything that happens to us is managed by God. Our highs and lows. Our mistakes and troubles. The pain of everything that goes wrong. God manages all of this, and is guiding us to where he wants us to be.

We should lean on God heavily, for our comfort and peace. We shouldn't try to be happy based on what we do, or how far we get in life. That's not what life's about. Life's about love. And real love comes from God. He'll comfort us, no matter what happens in our lives. He'll be by our side, even if we make a lot of mistakes. God loves us, as we are. He's our true comfort.

We're Forgiven

We've been forgiven everything. We've been forgiven everything.

Every bad word. Every bad thought. All of our mistakes. Every time we've let someone down. Every time we haven't done enough. Haven't done what we should. Every part of ourselves that is lacking. Every error. Every mistake. Every fault. Every sin.

We've been forgiven everything. Completely. We're not held at fault, for everything that's wrong with us. We're not held at fault, for everything about us that's not good enough. That's less than it should be. Jesus has forgiven us, and looks at us with a love so great that it wipes out all of the pain and misery in our lives.

It's not that Jesus doesn't see our problems; our mistakes and faults. He does. But he loves us so much, that he took the blame for everything that's wrong with us, and wrong in our lives. He died for us. He loves us so much, that rather than have us suffer alone, and pay for our sins ourselves, he died to pay for them.

He wants to give us a gift — the gift of life. The gift of love. He couldn't bear to see us struggling, and suffering alone. So he took responsibility — the blame, for every dark thing in our lives. In the world. He wiped the dark things out. We're debt free. We're sin free. We're free.

Never forget you've been forgiven. That you're not alone, with the problems that plague you. With the negativity that keeps a hold of you. You're not alone. You're not abandoned. You're not by yourself. And you're forgiven.

God Isn't Disappointed in Us

God's heart bursts with love. He feels such compassion, such love, grace and mercy. He can't wait to help us. He's desperate to look after us, provide comfort, and be by our side. God loves us so much. We're treasured, and smiled upon.

The thing that breaks God's heart, is that we feel he's upset with us. He's heartbroken that we feel guilty or ashamed in his presence — that we feel he's angry with us. God loves everyone with a strong, pure love, and is always by our side.

God's greatest desire is not that we become pure beings, who never sin. God's greatest desire is for us to know the depth of his love. For us to be happy, and free, and at peace. He wants us to feel comforted and safe.

The greatest barrier between us and God is thinking he's disappointed in us. That he expects us to behave differently, or give certain things up. We think he's angry if our focus isn't constantly on him. We feel he's upset we're not completely filled with love for him at all times.

God would have to be terrible to think of us this way. He just feels love. He's not ashamed or disappointed with everyone. He's not ashamed. He sees the good in us, the good that we never see. We judge ourselves far more harshly than God ever would. He's only about love. He loves us.

Rest in the peace of God's love. Know he thinks the best of you, no matter how you feel. He sees you as precious. If you feel that God is judging you, it's not from God. He doesn't judge. He loves you.

We Don't Have an Obligation

Sometimes I feel God makes certain things happen in my life. Once, when I was unemployed, I got a job right when I was about to run out of money. Everything came together at once, and I felt very strongly God had placed me in that position. I felt he wanted me to have that job, and it was important for me to be there.

It was good, at first. Then it was awful. Low pay, too much responsibility, no help, and employers who were extremely critical. It was so difficult, and made me miserable. I didn't know what to do.

The obvious answer was to try to get another job, but I felt conflicted. I felt God had placed me there — wouldn't he expect me to stay? Wasn't I meant to wait for God to fix things? Wasn't I supposed to have faith God would lead the situation where it was meant to go? I felt I was supposed to stay. I felt very upset that God had given me a job in which I became miserable. It caused a big conflict between me and God.

In the end, things became really bad, and I was fired. On one hand, I can see important things I learned about life and myself while I was there. I can see how I was meant to be in that job, for a time. But I tortured myself over whether to stay in a job, that I was going to lose anyway. The pain I felt over whether I had to stay in the job to please God was really hard to deal with.

I've since learned that God doesn't have specific standards for what he wants us to do. There's no invisible set of rules, no obligation for us to behave a certain way, or else God will be disappointed in us.

God loves us. Even if he leads us somewhere for a specific purpose, it doesn't mean we can't leave if we feel we should.

That specific purpose could have been fulfilled in the first week. We don't know God's reasons, or his timing. He brings us where we need to be, but we shouldn't feel we're doing something against God if we leave. It may be God's intention for us to leave at that time. We just don't know.

We should follow our heart, and our mind. Do what we feel is right. God won't be angry with us. All he wants is for us to be happy. All he wants is to love us. Being a Christian can be very confusing. Try to remember God loves us at all times, and will never be angry with us for following our heart. He loves us.

God Sees Every Part of Me

I go through my life, and find so much of it a struggle. My emotions go up and down. I worry and stress about so much. And I always feel God is upset with me.

The separation I feel from God hurts the most. I feel I'm so broken; I feel that my thoughts are so horrible and wrong, that even God would reject me. I feel God stands back, disappointed in me. He doesn't see what's truly in my heart — if he did, he'd hate me.

God doesn't really know what's going on in my life. He couldn't possibly understand. All of his promises are for a purer person. All of his promises are for someone who's good. I don't feel I'm good. I feel I'm awful.

But God knows every inch of me. He sees every part of me — everything that's going on in my life. He sees every single aspect, good and bad. He promises to be in control. And he is in control, no matter how I feel, no matter what I'm going through, no matter how dark I feel inside.

Sometimes in life, we just have to keep going, despite feeling terrible. We can feel we're horrible people, and there's so much that's wrong with us. We can feel we're not coping, and doing everything wrong. But God sees all of this. God's promise of love and healing, doesn't mean we won't feel any pain. It doesn't mean we'll feel good, or even accepted. All we can really hold onto is that his promises are true. And try to keep going.

The peace I feel in times of turmoil is knowing that God sees all of my pain and darkness, and is still guiding and leading me. I may feel awful, but God is in control of my life. He sees all of my problems, and is carefully managing everything. My problems aren't because I'm a bad person, or a stupid person. Everything that happens in my life is controlled by God. God's even in control of my relationship with him. All I can do, is keep going. That's all I can do.

God loves me, even when I don't love myself. God loves me despite the darkness inside of me. He's in control of my life, no matter how terrible I feel. He's managing everything. All I can do is keep working, and hold on. Hold on.

GOD WANTS TO HEAL OUR RELATIONSHIPS

What does God expect of us in our relationships? I feel I need to behave well, and be insightful about my relationships. I need to understand everything properly, and do the right thing. Things need to be okay.

God embraces us with a pure love, which covers our lives and makes us whole. On our own, we're sad and broken. On our own, we're relying on our own strength. It's up to us to fix everything. It's up to us to heal ourselves, and others.

But God wishes to heal us. Jesus sits beside us, holding our hand, taking care of everything in our lives. He wants to heal our relationships. He wishes to calm and reassure us — to change our hearts from sadness and bitterness, to love and peace. God wants to take care of us. God does take care of us.

The peace offered by Jesus isn't bound by rules or expectations. He doesn't expect us to think or behave a certain way, to help us. We just need to be with him, even by the smallest amount. Jesus embraces us. He rests a hand on our shoulder, telling us things will be okay. He wants us to feel calm. He wants to love us.

It's not up to us to fix everything. Release your burden to Jesus. Don't feel you need to carry the weight of your problems on your own. Jesus holds onto you. He's with you. He won't leave you alone, to manage your pain by yourself. He carries us. He carries us.

Release your burden to Jesus. You don't have to heal your relationships on your own. You don't have to take care of everything on your own. Just be with God; pray to him, hold firm to him, and remember he completely loves you. Jesus loves us. He'll take care of us. He's always with us.

GOD'S EXPECTATIONS

I keep thinking God expects a lot of me. I think that, in my troubles, God wants me to think very clearly, and do all the right things. Manage everything well. I believe God wants me to act carefully, and be completely responsible. Be the best I can be.

I'm underestimating God's power, if I think he can't rescue me from my troubles, unless I'm behaving properly. I'm reducing how powerful he is in my mind, if I think his actions to heal me are based on my actions.

Whilst I do believe God wants us to make an effort, he won't ignore us or step back from us if we're not doing enough. I tell myself I need to be some kind of super woman, who follows up every lead and does everything possible to heal my situations. I tell myself I should take care of EVERYTHING, and if I haven't, then maybe I haven't done what God wanted. Maybe I let him and those I love down. If things go horribly wrong, it's my fault.

But God's much sweeter than that. He's much more generous and loving than that. I don't need to be a super woman. I don't need to be perfect. God's actions aren't based on my actions. I'm allowed to fall apart. I'm allowed to be ordinary.

No one can do everything exactly right; we can't tell ourselves we need to manage everything perfectly, or else the consequences are our fault. We're only human. Do what you can. But God won't stand over us, not helping unless we've met certain criteria.

God will help us, and have a plan for us, on his own. He'll help us on his own. God is in control. He doesn't need us to do all the right things, to help us. We can fall apart. We can be ordinary. We can sit in our room and cry, overwrought with all of our problems. God doesn't want us to be more than we are. He'll take care of us. We only need to relax, and be ourselves. God will look after us.

Why It Has to Rain

There are certain types of problems for which the answer isn't doing a specific thing. It's not about us behaving a certain way, thinking a certain way — in fact, there's nothing we can do. The situation is just terrible. There's no clear answer, and sometimes removing ourselves from the situation isn't possible. The only solution is the problem being rectified by something beyond us. Something big has to happen, which we can't manage.

In my life, it's God who stops my pain. My faith is quite small in my troubled times, and I don't see how God can fix things. I don't believe very strongly that he'll make the situation better. I'm distressed, almost beyond what I can handle.

But God does rescue me. It's his power that makes things improve. I wish, very sincerely, that God would help me sooner. I become very sad, and wish I wasn't pushed to my limit. But God does rescue me. It's God who saves me. I can't save myself. I just can't. It's God who saves me.

What can I say to those who suffer, with no end in sight? I feel your pain, and know what it's like to be angry with God in these times. He's our savior, yet he makes us wait. The waiting is horrible.

But he will rescue us. It's not about us — our power. Our strength can't take this pain away. It's not about thinking exactly right, or doing all the right things. As unfortunate as it may be, sometimes we need to suffer in our lives, but God is in control of every moment of our suffering. We can't take it away ourselves. We'll be in pain as long as is necessary, as long as God has designed.

I'll always stay with God, and try to remember everything I go through has a higher purpose. God does love us, and wants what's best for us. If a thousand sunny days was best for us, God would provide that. But sometimes it has to rain. No one likes the rain. But without rain, nothing can grow.

JESUS SEES EVERYTHING THAT'S GOOD ABOUT US

Jesus loves me. I had a dream, in which he said he was proud of me. He viewed me as strong, and independent, and capable of looking after myself. He said I was able to figure things out on my own, and that's why he didn't spell things out for me all the time. I was able to cope with many things, and, even in the darkest of situations, I would be strong and able to manage. He was proud of me, and thought well of me. He was proud of me.

I forget Jesus views us individually. I think Jesus looks at all people the same, and doesn't see our individuality and strengths. We're all the same to him. We're just meant to be used for his good. We all blend in as one.

But Jesus looks at each person separately. I think Jesus can't look at me too closely, because he's blotting out my sins. If he's not seeing my sins, then he can't see my strengths, either. If he doesn't see the bad, he can't see the good.

But Jesus does see our faults and sins — all of them. He sees our sins, then lovingly forgives us. His forgiveness is not like an automatic response, because he has to. He looks at us kindly, and gently, and softly, and tells us he forgives us. He doesn't become angry with us. He knows why we did what we did.

Just as he looks at us closely to forgive us, he also closely sees our strengths. He sees everything that's good about us — any time we've been kind, any time we've coped with something difficult, any time we've persevered through failure. He sees all of our good points. He loves us for who we are, not because he has to. Jesus' love is no less individual or specific for us, just because he loves everyone. He would have died for you, if you were the last person on earth. His death was for you. He's here for you.

Jesus sees everything that's good about us. He loves us.

The Question of Church

I've seen it written many times that you can't be a Christian unless you go to church. People say, repeatedly, that you can't be an effective Christian unless you're part of a group of Christians, and quote Bible verses to reiterate this. They make it sound as if, if you don't go to church, you'll be separate from God. God won't be with you. You won't be able to grow as a Christian.

But I don't go to church. I have, in the past, many times, but I stopped going a long time ago. And I'm with God more now than I ever was before.

I'm not saying no one should go to church — it helps a lot of people. If people can find joy, and love, and learn something there, great. But I'm fiercely against the notion that if you don't go to church, you can't be a Christian. It doesn't make sense. It goes against everything God is about.

God is about love. I stopped going to church because, no matter which one I attended, the sermons were rarely about God's love and acceptance. The sermons were often about how to obey God better, and admonished people for not living up to a Godly standard.

I stopped going to church because, despite the fact that I'm shy and find it hard to talk to people, I was thrust into an environment where I was expected to be friendly and outgoing. I was frowned upon if I just wanted to sit by myself and listen quietly.

Churches often place rules and expectations on people. You must be friendly. You must love others. You must love God. You must obey rules. You must follow principles. You must give, even when you have nothing to give. You have to be in a certain place with God, emotionally and intellectually.

You have to do the right thing. You have to do the right thing.

But I've learned, over many years, that God expects none of this. God just wants to love us, as we are. Broken, lonely, alone, miserable. God's with us, and takes us as we are. Even if we never set foot in a church.

What matters is where our heart is. Do we want to be with God? All God wants is for us to be with him, even if we do very little. All God wants is for us to stay with him, and try. He just wants us to try.

I've grown close to God over the years, because God has brought me close to him. All I've done is stay with him, and I have gotten through my struggles and challenges as best I could. I'm by no means a perfect Christian, but I try, and I know God loves me and is proud of me. God truly loves and accepts me, no matter what I do.

I'm not saying to avoid church. Try it, if you've never tried it before. You may find it leads you to become closer to God, and feel less lonely. But if it goes against your heart and soul to go there — if you hate the thought of going — you don't have to go. Be with God in your home, in your own way. Learn about God the way you'd learn about anything you want to know about. Read about him, talk to him, write about him — whatever you want to do.

There's no exact thing to do. No exact way to be. Read the Bible sometimes. Read it to learn about God, not because you feel it's your duty. Be yourself. God would never want you to try to follow him in a way that makes you uncomfortable. All God wants, is your heart. And to love you.

GOD DOESN'T PRESSURE US

I remember feeling very uneasy when I first became a Christian. It wasn't just that it was new and confusing — I felt a pressure, as if God were watching me and expected me to behave a certain way. I felt as if I couldn't just live my life as I had been — study the course I was in, go home, talk to my friends. I felt a pressure. I was supposed to think or feel differently.

To an extent, I still feel that pressure. I've learned a lot about God, and how much he loves and accepts us. I've grown a lot as a Christian. However, I still feel God is watching me, expecting me to meet certain standards of living. I can't just relax, and be me.

All of these thoughts — these worries, concerns, nervous feelings — come from not seeing how much God loves me. Not knowing what he's really like. When I truly sense God's presence — in those few, precious moments — I feel so much better.

I realize he's my best friend. A best friend who sits by my side and tells me I'm alright. A best friend who always holds onto me, and never leaves me to struggle alone. I realize God is warm, comforting and kind, and never frowns upon me.

God wants me to relax and enjoy my life. It's not that he's upset with me if I become stressed, as if he's disappointed in me for working too hard, and wishes I would calm down. He never frowns upon me. He isn't disappointed in me, one way or the other — if I'm extremely stressed, or if I haven't worked very hard that day. God loves me, as I am.

God doesn't have a "checklist," where he wants us to do certain things or think a particular way. He doesn't stand over us, thinking we're not good enough. He completely loves us as we are.

The overall goal of Christianity is not to think or behave a certain way. It's to know God loves us, and feel accepted and nurtured. If we felt loved by God, we would naturally grow closer to him. If we grew closer to him, we would become more like Christ.

Don't tell yourself the goal of your Christianity is to change as a person. Tell yourself all God wants is to love and accept you. He'd love you if you never changed at all. He'd love you if you did everything wrong, and were selfish and unkind.

God loves you, as you are. It's thinking he doesn't love us, that causes the problems.

God is Only About Love

Imagine if God stood by our side when we worked, and was pleased with how we coped with things. Instead of wishing we would pay more attention to him. Instead of frowning upon us for not focusing on him all the time.

He is pleased with us. He does stand by our side.

Imagine if God didn't stand back from us, thinking we're not pure enough of heart, telling us our intentions aren't good enough. Telling us we should be good and kind and wholesome at all times.

God isn't like that. He accepts us as we are.

And what if God thought well of us, and was pleased with us when we worked hard? If he was proud of what we did for a living, even if it had nothing to do with him? Was pleased if we worked well, even if we didn't save people?

God *is* proud when we work hard. We don't have to evangelize for him all the time. We can just be ourselves.

God is completely good. Completely kind. He loves us without judgment.

He thinks the best of us, like a loving best friend. He always sees our good side, and nurtures and reassures us.

He doesn't have expectations, judgments, structures, rules. All he wants to do is love and help us. Love and help us.

God is only about love. He's completely good and perfect. There's nothing about God that's judgmental or unkind. Nothing that's disapproving or harsh.

God is only about love. We tell ourselves otherwise. We're told otherwise, and believe otherwise. But if we try to believe the truth — try to find the *truth* — we'd discover a God who's completely loving and kind, and only has our best interests at heart. He isn't mad at us. He isn't upset with us. He doesn't think badly of us.

God is only about love. It needs to be said, over and over, until we can't imagine otherwise.

God is Our Closest Friend

I'm an ordinary person. Sometimes I'm selfish and unkind. Sometimes I want to put myself first. When I work, I want to succeed, and my entire focus will be on my work at that time. I don't always want to give. My heart isn't always pure. I'm an ordinary person. And my heart is ordinary.

God isn't disappointed in me, because of this. God looks at me fondly. He looks at me with love and kindness. He isn't disappointed in me, wishing my heart were purer, wishing I was kinder and more selfless. God loves and accepts me as I am.

I've lately thought of God as a best friend, not just a loving parent. If you imagine a best friend, they sympathize with what you're going through. They won't say: "You should be more selfless. You should think about that differently. You're not good enough."

If your best friend spoke to you that way, you wouldn't want to be around them anymore, because they wouldn't be offering love and support. God isn't like this. He sits with us, and, like a true friend, completely understands our heart and soul. He understands when we're hurt and frustrated. He understands our desire to be selfish sometimes. He understands, and *doesn't judge us*.

God loves us, completely. When we realize God is completely loving, accepting and kind — when we realize he loves us, as we are — we feel so much closer to him. When we feel closer to him, we naturally want to do things to make him happy. Becoming a kinder, more giving person doesn't come from guilt, or being told we should be different. Becoming kinder comes from our heart. Comes from our heart, when it's filled with love. God's love.

Don't ever feel God's standing over you, wishing you would become more selfless and behave differently. God loves and accepts you as you are. He sees everything we're going through — every single detail — and is completely understanding and sympathetic. Even if we're going through dark things. Even if we've done dark things. God will never walk away from us. He never would, and never will.

God loves us, as we are. He understands. He forgives every bad thing we've ever done. He'll never leave us. He loves us.

Jesus Sees Us As Blameless

Jesus doesn't see us as flawed and a mess. He doesn't hold things against us — he doesn't look at us badly, for all of our errors, mistakes and inadequacies. His blood has washed us clean. He sees us as blameless, and beautiful; lovely and kind. He looks at us with love. He loves us.

Jesus doesn't blame us for what we do wrong. He isn't disappointed or ashamed of us. He doesn't think of us badly, holding back his blessings because of our mistakes. He doesn't frown upon us if we don't do well enough, or fail, or are grossly behind other people. He's completely happy with us, at all times, as he sees into our heart and soul. He loves us. He's proud of us. He only wants to rescue and bless us.

We can fail, fall behind, look foolish before others; we can make a million mistakes and be confused, anxious and stressed. We can do badly and be hated by everyone, or feel terrible and as if we're doing everything wrong. Jesus still loves us. Loves us, and sees us as *blameless*.

Jesus doesn't see the darkness we think hangs over us. The deep shame we think follows us everywhere, because we're flawed. Jesus doesn't look at us that way. He doesn't see that darkness. He's sitting right beside us, loving and giving to us completely, no matter how horrible we feel.

There's no barrier between us and God. There's nothing we can do to separate God's love from us. No matter how we feel, Jesus loves us. No matter what we do — how much we think we've ruined our lives — Jesus is still with us, seeing us as *blameless*, loving us completely. Jesus' blood has washed us clean. There's *nothing* we can do to separate ourselves from God. Jesus is always with us. Jesus will always bless us. He'll always see us as beautiful. No matter how messed up we are.

We're Acceptable Because of Jesus

It's not that I'm okay if my sin is understandable, or I can compare myself to others and seem alright. It's that I'm okay because Jesus has died for my sin — taken the *blame* for my sin — so I'm good enough because God makes me so.

It's not that I'm good enough because I haven't crossed a threshold of wrongdoing, and gone over into a "bad place." It's that I'm good enough because, no matter *what* my transgression, Jesus has died for it, and paid my penalty. No matter how dark my sin — no matter *what* I've done, Jesus has taken the blame for it, and washed me clean.

Jesus sees our sins before we do them. He anticipates them. He's prepared for them. He's *already* died for them — already suffered, and been physically tortured, for us. The intense pain he suffered, was for us. He's already paid for our sins. All of them.

We're not okay because we do okay. Our goodness, and acceptance by God, and *relationship* with God, isn't based on our behavior. As if, if we aren't good, it all ends. Our goodness, and acceptance by God, and *relationship* with God, is based on Jesus' sacrifice and love for us.

Jesus has paid for every bad thing we've done, and will do. He's paid for all of it. He's paid for every bad thing we've done, and *will do*. His blood has washed us clean. We're not alone any more.

Being good enough doesn't rest on our shoulders — what we do. We're acceptable because of Jesus. Not us. It was never about us. We couldn't be good enough if we tried. All we can do is get through each day, and trust that Jesus is purifying and cleansing us as we ask for forgiveness.

Jesus sees our sins before we do them. He's already suffered for them. We can't surprise him. If we're suffering — if we *hate* ourselves, and feel full of shame and misery, Jesus is controlling it. It's not our fault. We're only suffering to the measures he allows. It's not on our shoulders to fix ourselves. It's not on our shoulders to be good. Jesus controls that. He manages it.

Our goodness is controlled by Jesus. We're okay because of him. We're okay because he's okay. And he'll always be okay.

JESUS UNDERSTANDS OUR SIN

I feel as if Jesus doesn't understand the magnitude of what I do wrong. That, although he forgives me, he doesn't get it. He doesn't get what I did. How can his forgiveness make me clean? I feel so dirty inside. How can he have forgiven me? Doesn't he get that I did something BAD? Doesn't he get that I did something UGLY? He's not with me, in the mess. He doesn't feel what I feel. He doesn't see what I've done. Just because he doesn't hold it against me, doesn't mean there still isn't a black scar against my heart. My heart remembers. I hold it against me, even if he doesn't.

But Jesus controls everything about us — everything we do, everything that happens to us, everything that goes wrong. It's not that when we do the wrong thing, we've broken away from him, and we're out of his reach. That because we did the wrong thing, we turned our back on him, and he can't see us. He can't look at us. We've broken the bond.

Jesus controls EVERYTHING in our lives, so, even when we do something horrible, he's right there with us. Nothing is out of his control. Even the bad, ugly, terrible thing, is managed by him. He saw it before we did it. He saw our heart — our soul, our pain, our anguish — and was right there in the moment with us. He understands. He understood.

God loves us, as we are. He doesn't condone wrongdoing — he takes sin so seriously, that it took Jesus' death to make up for it. But, because of Jesus' death, God doesn't hold our sin against us. And, because of his love, he doesn't think badly of us. God forgives our sin because of Jesus. But he loves us, and forgives, understands, blesses and treasures us, because we're his children. Because he loved us from the moment we existed. Because he has always loved us, even before we were Christians.

God loves us, as we are. Because of Jesus' sacrifice, he'll control every single thing in our lives — what we do, and what happens to us. We're not alone, anymore. We're not alone anymore.

Nothing is out of Jesus' control. He controls our sin, and the consequences; he controls our pain and misery. Our pain is not our fault. Jesus is controlling it. He'll take it away, when it's right for him. Our suffering is not our fault. It's not as if, we feel badly because what we did was so horrible, that God has looked away from us. Jesus controls our sin, and our pain afterward. He's managing all of it. Nothing is out of his hands.

God loves us. Nothing we can do could separate us from him. And he does get it. He made us. He gets it.

God is Proud of How We Work

When I'm working, all I can think about is what I'm doing wrong. The tasks I'm not achieving. The standards I'm not reaching. The goals and milestones I'm nowhere near. All I can think is, *If only I could work better. If only I were smarter, more capable, and could do everything the way the others do. Everyone seems to be doing better than I'm doing.*

But Jesus doesn't look at us this way. He looks at what we've done — what we're doing — and is so proud. He doesn't see what we've done as inadequate or less than it should be. Jesus sees how hard we've worked, and the intention behind our work. God himself is proud of us, proud that we've tried, and that we meant well. That's what matters to God. Not that we've achieved what people say we should.

God loves us, so much. If God has a plan for us, he'll fulfil it, in his way. We have a part to play, but it's not as if we have to meet a certain standard, or we've failed God. That we've let God down, and he can't do what he wanted to do.

Nothing can stop God. All he asks of us is to try, and try to have good intentions. Try to do the right thing. It doesn't matter to God if we're far behind those we're competing with — if, compared to others, we're not working at the same level. None of that is relevant to God. He just wants us to try. Our heart and soul is what matters, and that we've done what we could. God will do the rest.

Nothing can stop God. God will never say our work isn't good enough — that we should have worked harder, or done more. We just have to do what we can. God's power and strength will make up for what we lack. He'll fill in what we leave out. He'll protect us. He holds us so closely.

God loves us, as we are. Not only if we do well.

God Controls Our Lives

Even if we feel alone and abandoned, God is with us. Even if we feel completely far from him, and as if we're not connected to him at all, he's still carefully watching us, and carefully managing our lives. God being active in our lives isn't based on our actions. It's not as if, if we don't do enough, or don't think of him properly, that he becomes separated from us.

God completely loves us, as we are. We can feel very uncomfortable, disoriented, and confused, as when we go through a major change in our lives. God is still with us, even if we feel terrible. Feeling great discomfort and anxiety doesn't mean God is separate from us. He controls everything.

We don't have to be strong and behave perfectly in our times of distress, for things to work out the way God has planned. He's always in control. Even if we've done the wrong thing. Even if we feel we're not good enough.

God doesn't frown upon us, thinking we're horrible people if we're selfish sometimes, or don't know how to care for others properly. God will help us care for others. He'll help us to do the right thing. Everything doesn't fall on our shoulders.

God loves us. He'll protect and help us. He'll never leave us alone, no matter how we feel, or what we've done. We're not alone.

JESUS WILL ALWAYS FORGIVE US

I forget that, because Jesus died for me, that all of my sins are forgiven. I feel as if I taint things — that because I make bad choices or decisions, or can be selfish, I destroy things so badly that Jesus can't look at me. He can't forgive me.

But Jesus died for me. He was killed, for me. Nothing can separate us.

I feel if I'm not sorry enough for my sins, if I don't do enough to change what I've done, then God is far from me. I feel Jesus' forgiveness of my sins is *entirely* based on me rectifying the situation. It's not enough for me to be sorry. It's not enough for me to want to change — to want to do the right thing. I have to earn Jesus' forgiveness.

But God forgiving me is based on the fact that Jesus died for me. He took the blame for what I do wrong. It's not that God forgives me based on what my sin is, or what I've done to make up for it. God's forgiveness of me is *entirely* based on Jesus' sacrifice. My debt has been paid.

God will never hold our sins against us. There's nothing we could do, that would be so bad that the death of God himself would not be enough to make up for it. Jesus treasures us. If we aren't doing enough to rectify the bad situation we're in, Jesus forgives that too. There's no limit to how much God forgives us. *There's no black scar against our heart.* Jesus will always forgive us. He'll help us make things right.

Jesus loves us, as we are. He'll always hold onto us very closely. And he'll never let go.

How Much Jesus Loves You

Jesus' love for us is pure, and real, and strong. It's such an intense love — it's the kind of love we usually only dream about. Jesus loves us with such passion, and cares for us more deeply than we could ever imagine. He craves looking after us. He's immensely dedicated to caring for us, and our welfare. He loves us so strongly. He loves us so deeply.

Jesus is entirely on our side. Every single one of us. *Entirely* on our side. When we argue with someone, he looks at us fondly, thinking we shouldn't have been treated that way. He wants things to work out for us — he'll work hard to make things work our way. He wants us to be comforted and safe. He wants us to be free and at peace.

Jesus loves us so deeply. He's our best friend. Imagine the kind of love you crave. Imagine that kind of intense love. Someone you can share your fears with. Someone who'll listen to your every worry and concern. Someone who'll be by your side in everything you go through. Who tells you you *are* good enough. You *are* doing enough. You are good enough. You are doing enough.

Someone who loves you. Who won't leave you to manage things on your own. Who says: "If you don't have the strength, I'll do it. You don't have to be incredibly strong. I'm with you. I'll be strong enough for both of us. I'll be your strength."

Imagine somebody who forgives every bad thing you do, forgives every time you didn't do enough, and tells you they understand. They would say: "You had a reason. You're not a bad person, at all. I know why you did what you did. I know why you let that person down. It's not your fault. You are good enough. You did what you could."

Someone who loves you more than they value their life. Who would give up everything for you.

Imagine that kind of love. That's how much Jesus loves you.

God Will Change Our Lives

Sometimes we can be in a bad situation, and can't see our way out. We make plans to change things, but acting out the plans seems excruciating, and we don't know what to do. We feel we have to force our lives to be better — do very difficult, painful things, to make our situation improve. We feel so lost and alone. It's such a miserable situation to be in.

What I've learned is that God will come through for us. It may be months in the future, in a way we don't expect, but God will heal and transform our lives. God doesn't want us to stress, worry or be concerned; he doesn't want us to feel we have to control everything. He'll be in control. He'll improve our lives.

The immense pressure I feel, thinking I have to make my life better, and if I'm miserable it's my own fault — none of that's true. God is managing my life.

It's not as if God's waiting for me to behave a certain way, so he can help me. As if I need to behave perfectly and appropriately, doing everything correctly, or he can't act. No matter what I do, no matter how big a mess I make of things, or how foolish and inadequate I feel, God is in control.

Don't feel you're inadequate, and God can't help you because of it. Nothing can stop God. He sees everything that's good about you, and will help you according to the plan he has laid out. He loves you. God can achieve any positive outcome. He'll take care of you. He loves you.

About the Author

Mona Hanna is the author of the books "The Nature of God" and "God's Promises of Love." She has been a devotional writer since 2008, creating the blog Mona Hanna Devotions, focusing on expressing God's love, acceptance, and compassion. She has a Bachelor of Arts degree from the University of South Australia, with a sub major in professional writing. She has worked in the private and public sectors, and is now committed to communicating the lessons she learns from her personal walk with Christ.

Mona's devotions break down the notion that God judges us, and has strict requirements for how we should think, feel and behave. Her stance is that God loves us as a parent loves their child, with the same intimacy, compassion, and knowledge of every part of our lives, which a loving parent would have. The devotions portray God's immense love for us, his kindness, sweetness, grace, mercy, forgiveness, and generosity.

monahannadevotions.com